LAND LAW

The University of Law

LAND LAW
FIFTH EDITION

Kate Lambert

This edition published 2025 by
The University of Law
2 Bunhill Row
London EC1Y 8HQ

British Library Cataloguing in Publication Data

A catalogue record for this book is available from the British Library.

ISBN 978 1 80502 262 6

Preface

This book is part of a series of Study Manuals that have been specially designed to support the reader to achieve the SQE1 Assessment Specification in relation to Functioning Legal Knowledge. Each Study Manual aims to provide the reader with a solid knowledge and understanding of fundamental legal principles and rules, including how those principles and rules might be applied in practice.

This Study Manual covers the Solicitors Regulation Authority's syllabus for the SQE1 assessment for Land Law in a concise and tightly focused manner. The Manual provides a clear statement of relevant legal rules and a well-defined road map through examinable law and practice. The Manual aims to bring the law and practice to life through the use of example scenarios based on realistic client-based problems and allows the reader to test their knowledge and understanding through single best answer questions that have been modelled on the SRA's sample assessment questions.

For those readers who are students at the University of Law, the Study Manual is used alongside other learning resources and the University's assessment bank to best prepare students not only for the SQE1 assessments, but also for a future life in professional legal practice.

We hope that you find the Study Manual supportive of your preparation for SQE1 and we wish you every success.

The legal principles and rules contained within this Manual are stated as at 1 May 2025.

Author acknowledgments
Kate would like to thank Helen Avis, the previous author, for her considerable work in the writing of this book. Thanks must also go to David Stott for his editorial support and guidance.

Contents

Table of Cases

Table of Statutes

1 The Nature of Land

SQE1 syllabus

Nature of land:

- Distinction between real property and personal property
- How to acquire and transfer legal and equitable estates
- How to acquire and dispose of legal and equitable interests in land
- Different ways in which land can be held
- Legal formalities required to create and transfer interests and estates in land

Note that for SQE1, candidates are not usually required to recall specific case names or cite statutory or regulatory authorities. Cases are provided for illustrative purposes only.

Learning outcomes

By the end of this chapter you will be able to apply relevant core legal principles and rules appropriately and effectively, at the level of a competent newly qualified solicitor in practice, to realistic client-based and ethical problems and situations in the following areas:

- Explain the key definitions on the meaning of land
- Distinguish between a fixture and a chattel
- Identify estates in land
- Identify interests in land
- Explain how estates and interests in land are validly created and transferred.

1.1 Introduction to the nature of land

Land Law has a reputation for being a difficult subject to study. Land Law is not so easy to relate to as, say, Criminal Law or Tort. Studying Land Law therefore needs a slightly different approach (see below). The rules relating to Land Law have developed over hundreds of years and use some antiquated language. A glossary is set out below to explain some of the key concepts and introduce some of the terminology. Each chapter will contain an explanation of the terminology used in each topic.

In this manual case law is referred to. You do not need to learn the names or facts of the cases. Focus instead on learning the principles derived from each case.

1.1.1 How to approach the study of Land Law

Set out below are some suggestions which may help:

(a) The essential basics and formalities in this chapter provide the building blocks for an understanding of the subject. It may appear procedural, but you will be unable to answer a question without this knowledge.

(b) Learn as you go and try not to compartmentalise your learning. Every topic you learn helps develop knowledge and understanding of the subject as a whole.

(c) Try to adopt a methodical approach. This involves unpacking a fact pattern and carefully considering how the rules apply.

(d) Accept that for every rule in Land Law there is usually an exception. You need to learn the rule and the exception(s).

(e) The enforcement of third-party rights in unregistered and registered land (in **Chapters 7 and 8** respectively) will make no sense unless you have an understanding of the contents of **Chapter 1**.

(f) The essential basics, formalities (**Chapter 1**) and third party rights (**Chapters 7 and 8**) relate to every other topic. **Chapter 9, Consolidation** provides guidance on how third party rights in registered and unregistered land fit into each topic covered in **Chapters 2 to 6**.

(g) Sometimes the rules/principles cannot be rationalised. This is usually where the law of equity has intervened to correct an injustice. The central principle of Land Law is that land should not be unnecessarily burdened.

(h) Expect it to take some time for the concepts and terminology to become familiar. Treat it like the study of a foreign language.

1.1.2 Glossary

An estate in land	A person with an estate in land has the right to enjoy, possess, control and dispose of it and receive any income produced from the land.
An interest in land	A person with an interest in land has a right against land owned by another person. For example, a right of way.
<u>Estates in land</u>	
Freehold	This is the freehold estate which lasts indefinitely. Its full legal name is 'fee simple absolute in possession'.

(*continued*)

Leasehold	This is the leasehold estate which lasts for a fixed period. Its full legal name is 'term of years absolute'. It is also described as a lease or tenancy. A freehold estate owner can grant a lease for any duration. A leasehold estate owner can only grant a sub-lease for a shorter duration than their own lease.
Interests in land	
Mortgage	An interest over land granted by the borrower to the lender as security for a loan. If the borrower fails to repay the loan, the lender can enforce its security.
Restrictive covenant	A promise by one landowner in favour of another landowner that they will not do certain things on the land. For example, not to use the land for any use other than a private home.
Easement	A right for one landowner to make use of another parcel of land for the benefit of their own land. For example, a right of way.
Profits	Or profits a prendre – a right to go on to somebody else's land and remove from the land something which exists naturally. For example, a right to catch and take fish or a right to graze animals.
Resulting trust	A person, who is not the legal owner, contributes directly to the purchase price of the property. The person acquires an interest proportionate to their contribution.
Constructive trust	An interest in land is created when a person, who is not the legal owner of the property, makes a contribution to the property other than a direct financial contribution at the time of the purchase. This can include contributing to the mortgage payments or making substantial improvements to the property.
Estate contract	A contract to convey or create a legal estate including an option to purchase. The sale and purchase of land normally has two stages. The first stage is when the seller and buyer enter into a contract in which it is agreed that the estate in land should be sold. Contracts are exchanged and the buyer holds an equitable interest. The second stage involves the seller transferring the property to the buyer. The sale is completed and the legal estate is transferred to the buyer. There is usually a short interval between the two stages. During that interval the buyer owns an estate contract (which is an equitable interest).
Option	An option enables the owner of the option to insist that the land is sold to them at any time during the fixed period of the option (the period must not exceed 21 years). An option fee is usually payable, but the full purchase price only becomes payable if the option is exercised. Options are a type of estate contract.
Statutory rights	
Home right	This is a statutory right for a non-owning spouse or civil partner to occupy the matrimonial home under the Family Law Act 1996. It does not create an interest in land.
Terminology	
Alienation	The sale or underletting of leasehold land.

(*continued*)

(*continued*)

Assignment	The transfer (or sale) of a lease between the tenant/lessee (an assignor) and a purchaser (an assignee).
Beneficial interest	The interest of a beneficiary under the trust (express, resulting or constructive).
Charge	An alternative word for a mortgage also expressed as a charge by way of legal mortgage.
Conveyance	A document transferring legal ownership in freehold unregistered land.
Dominant land	The land that benefits from a restrictive covenant or easement.
Fine	A sum of money paid to the landlord in return for granting a lease. Usually paid in addition to rent. Also known as a premium.
Fixed term lease	May be for any period of time as long as the maximum period is fixed.
Lessee/tenant	The owner of the leasehold estate.
Lessor/landlord	The person who grants the leasehold estate. The landlord retains the right to receive rent and sell the freehold (subject to the lease). The retained rights are known as the reversion.
Mortgagee	This is the lender who owns the mortgage interest in the land.
Mortgagor	This is the borrower, the person who owns the legal estate in land and grants the mortgage to the mortgagee (lender) as security for the loan.
Periodic lease	A lease for one period, which extends automatically until either the landlord or tenant give notice to quit. The period is usually a week, month or year.
Personal property	Rights in property except for land (goods and chattels).
Positive covenant	An obligation which requires effort or expenditure in order to perform the obligation.
Puisne mortgage	A legal mortgage over unregistered land which is not protected by the deposit of title deeds. Pronounced 'puny'.
Real property	All property rights relating to land (estates and interests, ie mortgages, easements etc).
Servient land	The land which is subject to or burdened by the covenant or easement. The easements are exercised over this land. The servient land is bound by the restrictive covenant.
Tenancy	This is the leasehold estate which lasts for a fixed period of time. Its full legal name is 'term of years absolute'. It is also described as a lease or leasehold. A freehold estate owner can grant a lease for any duration. A leasehold estate owner can only grant a sub-lease for a shorter duration than their own lease.
Time immemorial	1189 also known as the date of legal memory.
Transfer	A document transferring legal ownership in registered land.

1.2 What is land?

The meaning of land in an ordinary dictionary would say something like 'the solid part of the Earth's surface; ground; soil'. That is usually what we would imagine when we think of the ordinary meaning of the word 'land'. The legal definition of land is far broader and has multiple dimensions.

1.2.1 The statutory definition of land

Land is defined in s 205(1)(ix) of the Law of Property Act (LPA) 1925 as follows:

> Land includes land of any tenure, and mines and minerals, whether or not held apart from the surface, buildings or parts of buildings (whether the division is horizontal or vertical or made in any other way) and other corporeal hereditaments; also a manor, advowson, and a rent and other incorporeal hereditaments and an easement, right, privilege, or benefit in, over or derived from land...

This definition can be broken down as follows:

(a) The concept of tenure will be explained in **1.3** below.

(b) Mines and minerals would include, for example, any coal beneath the property. In practice, all interests in coal are now vested in the Coal Authority under the Coal Industry Act 1994.

(c) Corporeal hereditaments refer to the physical and tangible characteristics of land which are capable of being inherited. For example, trees, rocks and clods of earth.

(d) Incorporeal hereditaments are intangible property rights which are capable of being inherited. For example, profits and easements.

(e) The concepts of a manor and advowson reflect the feudal nature of the development of land law and have limited modern application.

(f) Buildings and parts of buildings are included within the definition of land. Buildings can be divided horizontally or vertically, meaning that it is possible for a building to be included within the definition of land although it does not touch the soil. This is called 'flying freehold'.

It is said that land extends upwards to infinity and downwards to the centre of the earth. There are modern limitations on this principle and the courts have sought to balance the rights of the landowner and those of the general public. This is particularly the case in relation to the use of airspace where a landowner's rights only extend to a height needed for ordinary use and enjoyment (*Bernstein v Skyviews & General Ltd* [1977] 3 WLR 136).

1.2.2 Fixtures are part of the land

Buildings and parts of buildings are included within the definition of land. What about items that are brought onto the land? A distinction is made between fixtures and chattels. Fixtures are included within the definition of land, whereas chattels retain their characteristic as personal property.

The distinction is important because when a landowner sells land, any fixtures must be passed to the buyer (unless the seller has made provision in the contract to remove such fixtures). The seller is entitled to retain and remove any chattels on the land.

The difficulty is that chattels can become fixtures. A good example is the analogy provided by Blackburn J in *Holland v Hodgson* LR 7 CP328:

> Thus blocks of stone placed one on the top of another without any mortar or cement for the purpose of forming a dry stone wall would become part of the land, though the same stones, if deposited in a builders yard and for convenience sake stacked on the top of each other in the form of a wall, would remain chattels.

The law has developed a two-stage test to determine whether an object is a fixture or a chattel (*Berkley v Poulett* [1977] 1 EGLR 86, CA):

(a) The degree of annexation; and

(b) The purpose of annexation.

The degree of annexation

How firmly affixed is the object to the land?

The object could be resting on the land by its own weight, for example, a sculpture. It may be attached to the land by means of battens (strips of wood) and screws, for example a picture or tapestry.

If the object cannot be removed without causing significant damage to the land, this indicates that it is a fixture; eg a fireplace, panelling or a conservatory. Conversely, if the object is easy to remove it would be easier to argue that it is a chattel; eg carpets or curtains. However, due to technological advances, objects can be affixed and removed from land or buildings with relative ease.

The degree of annexation is an initial test which raises a presumption that the item is a fixture, but the presumption can be rebutted.

The purpose of annexation

Why has the object been attached to the land?

This is the key test and takes priority over the degree of annexation.

If the object was attached to the land to enhance the land or to create a permanent improvement then it is a fixture. If the object was attached to the land for the better enjoyment of the object then it retains its characteristic as a chattel. The question depends on the circumstances of each case with the onus of proof being on the person claiming that the object has ceased to be a chattel. Examples from *TSB Bank Plc v Botham* [1996] EGCS 149 assist in understanding the two-stage test:

- Items which are ornamental are often chattels, for example pictures
- A free-standing cooker connected via a flex will be a chattel
- A split-level cooker with a built-in oven and inset hob will be a fixture as this would be difficult to remove without causing damage
- Kitchen units are fixtures
- Appliances in a kitchen can retain their characteristic as chattels as they are attached only by their weight and an electrical flex and can be removed or replaced without damage
- Items installed by a builder will probably be fixtures, for example wall tiles in a kitchen or bathroom
- Bathroom fittings (ie basins, baths and toilets) are fixtures as without them the room would not function as a bathroom
- Carpets and curtains are likely to be chattels
- A gas fire connected purely to function as a fire is likely to be a chattel
- Light fittings attached by screws are likely to be chattels.

The issue is less clear cut where there is an argument that the item attached to the land forms part of an architectural design. In *D'Eyncourt v Gregory* [1866] LR 3 Eq 382 tapestries fixed into panelled walls, pictures, marble vases and garden ornaments were held to be fixtures despite their ease of removal. This was due to the items being part of an overall architectural design.

It is possible for a chattel to become part of the land over time. For example, a mobile home resting on its own weight would retain its characteristic as a chattel if it was easy to remove. However, where a house is constructed in such a way that it cannot be removed at all, save by destruction, it has become a fixture as it is clearly intended to form part of the land (*Elitestone Ltd v Morris* [1977] 2 All ER 513).

Example 1.1

You act for Sam who has exchanged contracts for the purchase of 24 Lime Tree Avenue. Sam spoke to the seller earlier and is now concerned that the seller plans to remove a number of items that Sam thought would be included in the sale. Below is a list of the items. Can the seller remove them?

Item	Fixture (included in the sale)	Chattel (not included in the sale)
1. Carpets		
2. Pictures specially made for the living room decor		
3. Washing machine		
4. Split-level oven with inset hob		
5. Dilapidated greenhouse that is likely to fall to bits if moved		
6. Caravan		
7. A single statue of a large garden gnome resting by its own weight in the suburban garden		

Comment

Items 1, 3 and 6 have the character of chattels. None are firmly affixed to the land and the purpose of annexation is for the enjoyment of the object (*Botham*).

Unless item 7 forms part of an overall architectural design, it is likely to be a chattel. It is not affixed to the land and could be easily removed.

Item 4 is firmly affixed to the land and the purpose of annexation is for the better enjoyment of the land. It would be difficult to remove without causing damage. It is a fixture (*Botham*).

As it appears that the pictures in item 2 form part of an overall design, there is a stronger argument to suggest that they are fixtures (*D'Eyncourt v Gregory*).

A greenhouse (item 5) would usually be easy to move. However, the facts indicate that the greenhouse could not be moved without destruction. This would suggest that it is a fixture (*Elitestone*).

1.3 Tenure

Tenure has its roots in the feudal system developed following the Norman Conquest in 1066 when the king granted land to his supporters in return for their services. For example, a tenure in chivalry was by knight service. This has limited application since the implementation of the LPA 1925, which abolished the remaining medieval tenure (copyhold). There is now only one form of tenure, free and common socage (or freehold).

Technically, all land in England and Wales is held of the Crown. When we talk about 'ownership' of land we mean owning a bundle of rights in relation to the land. Scotland has its own distinct legal system.

1.4 Legal and equitable rights in land

Rights in land can be divided into two categories:

(a) Estates

(b) Interests

A number of people may have different, competing rights over the same land. For example:

- Mr Brown is the owner of a farm called Greenacre (freehold estate).
- He has granted a lease of a barn forming part of Greenacre to Mr Long (leasehold estate).
- He purchased Greenacre with the aid of a loan from Central Bank. Mr Brown has granted Central Bank a mortgage.
- He has granted his neighbour, Miss West, the right to walk across Greenacre to reach her beehives (easement).

In order to work out whether a buyer of Greenacre would be bound by these rights, you need to work out the following:

(a) What is the nature of the interest?

(b) Is the right legal or equitable?

(c) Has the right been protected?

Every property right (whether it is an estate or an interest) will either be legal or equitable. Only certain property rights can ever be legal, but all property rights are capable of being equitable.

The distinction is important because legal and equitable property rights are protected in different ways as you will see in **Chapters 7 and 8**.

A right will be legal if it:

(a) appears in ss 1(1) or 1(2) LPA 1925; and

(b) meets the necessary formalities.

Anything that falls outside of the list in ss 1(1) and (2) LPA 1925 can only be equitable – see s 1(3) LPA 1925. Equitable interests must also meet the necessary formalities.

1.5 Estates in land

The two estates that are *capable* of being legal are set out in s 1(1) LPA 1925:

(a) The estate in fee simple absolute in possession (freehold); and

(b) The term of years absolute (leasehold).

An estate is a period of time. A person owning an estate can create out of it a lesser estate, or shorter period of time. For example, a freehold owner can create a lease.

1.5.1 Freehold

An 'estate in fee simple absolute in possession' can be explained as follows:

- Fee means that the estate is capable of being inherited.
- Simple means that it can pass to any class of heir. It is unlikely that a person will die without any heir and therefore the estate is capable of lasting forever. The estate is akin to having permanent ownership of the land.
- Absolute indicates that the estate is not determinable or conditional on any event. For example, a conditional interest would be to A until they become a lawyer. Such an interest would now exist in equity.
- In possession means an immediate right to possession, rather than an entitlement to possession at some time in the future. For example, to A for life and then to B. B has no immediate right to possession. Such an interest would now exist in equity.

If a freehold owner dies with no will or heirs to inherit, the property reverts to the Crown.

1.5.2 Leaseholds

A lease is an estate in land where the tenant is granted exclusive possession of land for a fixed period. Unlike the freehold estate, a lease cannot last forever.

A lease is created or carved out of a superior interest, for example a freehold or longer lease. It is therefore possible to have more than one estate in relation to the same parcel of land; eg a freehold estate and a leasehold estate. This is reflected in s 1(5) LPA 1925.

Exclusive possession means the ability for the tenant to control the land and exclude everyone from the land, including the landlord.

'A term of years' is defined in s 205(1) LPA 1925 to include a term for less than a year, or for a year or years, and a fraction of a year or from year to year. This means that a lease can be of any duration.

There are two types of leases:

(a) fixed term; and

(b) periodic.

Fixed-term leases

A fixed-term lease can be for any period, provided that the maximum duration is certain; for example, one day, six months, an academic year or 999 years.

Periodic leases

A periodic lease is for one period (a fixed period), which goes on extending itself automatically until either the landlord or tenant terminates the lease by notice. The period can be weekly, monthly, yearly or any other period. Notice to quit would usually be for the period of the tenancy, ie one month for a monthly tenancy.

Example 1.2

Carl agrees to rent a garage from Lucy for one month. The parties are happy with the arrangement and the lease continues from month to month until either party ends it by notice. The lease can continue indefinitely until it is brought to an end by service of at least one month's notice.

1.5.3 Commonhold

The Commonhold and Leasehold Reform Act 2002 introduced a new form of freehold tenure, commonhold. This form of tenure gives a buyer a freehold interest in their flat or house with communal areas being managed by a commonhold association run by commonhold owners. Normally a buyer would acquire a lease of a flat with no guarantee of any involvement in the management of the communal areas. Commonhold therefore looks like an attractive alternative to granting a lease, but, as at 2023 (the latest figures available), only 184 commonholds had been registered at Land Registry in England and Wales which is less than 0.01% of the total number of properties in the same area. Commonhold may become popular in the future in light of the Government's proposed leasehold reforms.

1.6 Interests in land (capable of being legal)

A person who has an interest in land has a right over land owned by another person. These are set out in s 1(2) LPA 1925. They are capable of being legal provided the relevant formalities have been used. They are:

(a) Easements and profits

An easement is a right of one landowner to make use of another nearby piece of land for the benefit of their own land, for example a right of way.

A profit is a right to go on somebody else's land and take from that land something which exists naturally, for example a right to fish or a right to graze cattle.

Easements and profits are only capable of being legal if they are for a duration equivalent to an estate in fee simple absolute in possession (freehold) or a term of years absolute (leasehold). Only easements and profits lasting forever or for a fixed duration are capable of being legal. This means that an easement or profit for an uncertain duration is not capable of being legal.

(b) Rentcharges

A rentcharge is a right to receive a periodic payment charged on the land. They are uncommon. Rent charges are only capable of being legal if they are perpetual (ie forever) or for a term of years absolute (ie for a fixed duration).

(c) Charges by way of legal mortgage

A mortgage is an interest over property granted by the borrower to the lender as security for a debt or the discharge of some other obligation.

Although we say we are 'getting a mortgage' to purchase property, the lender provides a loan and in return the landowner grants the lender security by way of a mortgage over the property. The borrower is the mortgagor as they create the mortgage and the lender is the mortgagee as they have the benefit of the mortgage.

(d) Interests in land which arise by operation of statute

Some rights arise against a piece of land by operation of an Act of Parliament. The owner of the rights will, in practice, be some form of government agency. For example, the charge for inheritance tax or the charge for Legal Aid.

(e) Rights of entry

A right of entry is either:

- a landlord's right to forfeit the lease (bring the lease to a premature end) if the tenant breaks the terms of the lease; or
- a rentcharge owner's right to reclaim the land if the money owed is not paid.

The most important interests in land are easements and mortgages. Those are the interests that you will focus on.

1.7 Equitable interests in land

Whilst only certain property rights can be legal, all property rights are capable of being equitable.

Equitable property rights can be created in a number of different ways. The most significant are as follows:

- by contract to create or transfer a legal estate or interest
- by trying to grant a legal estate or interest but failing to comply with the relevant formalities
- by grant of an estate or interest by a person who owns only an equitable right
- by grant of an estate or interest which can only exist in equity
- by express trust
- by implied trust.

Express trust

Any type of property, including land, can be placed in a trust. A legal estate owner who creates an express trust is known as a settlor. A settlor may wish to create a trust to benefit their children.

The defining characteristic of the trust is that the legal title to the property is separated from the equitable interests. The person holding the legal title (freehold or leasehold) is known as the trustee. The person who is entitled to enjoy the benefits is known as the beneficiary. The trustees and the beneficiaries can be the same or different people.

Example 1.3

Adil is the freehold owner of Brook Mansion ('the Property'). Adil places the Property in trust for his five-year-old daughter, Maryam:

- *Adil is the trustee and holds the legal estate*
- *Maryam is the beneficiary.*

The common law has never recognised or protected the rights of a beneficiary. It only recognises and protects the rights of the person holding the legal estate, even if that person is holding the legal title for the benefit of someone else (the beneficiary). Equity intervened to protect the beneficiary through the device of a trust.

An express trust can be created by:

(a) self-declaration – here the settlor retains the legal title to their property but declares that they hold the property as trustee for the benefit of another person (the beneficiary); or

(b) declaration plus transfer – the settlor declares a trust and transfers legal title to their property to the trustees who hold the property for the benefit of the beneficiaries.

Implied trust

Trusts can arise impliedly without any express declaration of trust by the legal owner. There are two forms of implied trust:

- resulting; and
- constructive.

Resulting trust

A person who is not the legal owner contributes directly to the purchase price of the property. The person acquires an interest proportionate to their contribution.

Example 1.4

Dolly is the freehold owner of 24 Compton Road ('the Property'). Prior to the acquisition of the Property Dolly's mother, Enid, paid the 10 per cent deposit.

Enid made a direct contribution to the purchase price. This created a resulting trust, entitling her to 10 per cent of the value of the Property. This means that:

- *Dolly holds the legal estate of the Property as a trustee;*
- *The equitable (or beneficial) interest is held by Dolly (90%) and Enid (10%); and*
- *Dolly has a dual role as both a trustee and beneficiary.*

Constructive trust

An interest in land is created when a person, who is not the legal owner of the property, makes a contribution to the property other than a direct financial contribution at the time of the purchase. This can include contributing to the mortgage payments or making substantial improvements to the property. Unlike a resulting trust, the interest will not be proportionate to the contribution made, but quantified taking into account the parties' conduct, the direct and non-direct financial contributions and any non-financial contributions.

The most significant type of implied trust for trusts of the home is the constructive trust.

Example 1.5

Amanda is the freehold owner of 49 Hilton Crescent ('the Property'). Amanda therefore holds the legal estate.

Five years ago, Amanda's partner, Daniel, moved into the Property and has since paid half the mortgage payments and other outgoings. Daniel's conduct is sufficient to infer a common intention that Daniel holds a beneficial interest under a constructive trust. This means that:

- *the legal estate is held by Amanda as a trustee;*
- *the equitable (or beneficial) interest is held by Amanda and Daniel; and*
- *Amanda has a dual role as both a trustee and beneficiary.*

Interests equitable by nature

Some interests in land are equitable by nature. This is because they do not appear in s 1(1) or (2) LPA 1925. These include:

(a) A beneficial interest under a trust (whether express, implied, resulting or constructive).

(b) A restrictive covenant – this is a promise 'made' by one landowner (the covenantor) in favour of another landowner (the covenantee) that the covenantor will not use their land in a particular way. For example, not to use the property for any trade or business.

(c) An estate contract – the conveyancing process happens in two stages. In stage 1 the parties enter into a contract. In stage 2 title is transferred or a legal estate or interest is created (subject to the formalities set out at **1.10** below). There is usually a short period between stages 1 and 2. In this period the buyer holds an estate contract. This is recognised in equity only. It includes contracts for:

- the sale of a freehold or leasehold estate;
- an option (see glossary);
- a right of pre-emption (this is where a seller is obliged to offer their property to the buyer at the point that the seller decides to sell);
- the grant of a lease; and
- the grant of an easement or profit.

1.8 Statutory right

Section 30 of the Family Law Act (FLA) 1996 created 'home rights'. This is a statutory right of occupation of the matrimonial home for a non-owning spouse or civil partner. Non-owning means not holding the legal estate. The right arises provided that:

(a) the parties are legally married or civil partners (and not divorced); and

(b) the home is, has been or is intended to be the matrimonial home.

Home rights do not create an interest in land.

Home rights exist independently of any equitable interest arising under a trust (whether express or implied).

Example 1.6

Harriet is the freehold owner of 67 Hamlet Drive ('the Property'). Harriet's wife, Nicole, made a significant contribution to the purchase price of the Property.

What are Nicole's interests in the Property?

Comment

Nicole is the beneficiary under a resulting trust due to her significant contribution towards the purchase price. Harriet holds the legal estate as a trustee for herself and Nicole as beneficiaries.

Nicole does not hold the legal title to the Property and is therefore a non-owning spouse entitled to home rights.

1.9 Licence

A licence is a personal right and does not create an interest in land. This means that licences are binding only between the original parties and would not bind a successor in title.

The person granting the licence is the licensor and the person with the benefit of the licence is the licensee.

A licence is capable of authorising anything, from a simple right of access to temporary occupation as a lodger.

A licence can be revoked at any time.

Chapter 6 will consider the differences between a lease and a licence.

Example 1.7

Test your understanding by identifying which interests are capable of being legal and which are equitable by nature:

Interest	Capable of being legal	Equitable by nature
Mortgage		
Restrictive covenant		
Option to buy a freehold estate		
Easement for 20 years		
Contract for the sale of a freehold estate		
Easement for life		
Lease for five years		
Beneficial interest under a trust		
Contract to grant a legal easement		

Comment

Interest	Capable of being legal	Equitable by nature
Mortgage	A legal interest in section 1(2)(c) LPA 1925	
Restrictive covenant		It does not appear in s 1(1) or (2) LPA 1925 and is therefore equitable (s 1(3) LPA 1925)
Option to buy a freehold estate		It does not appear in s 1(1) or (2) LPA 1925 and is therefore equitable (s 1(3) LPA 1925)
Easement for 20 years	A legal interest in s 1(2)(a) LPA 1925	
Contract for the sale of a freehold estate		It does not appear in s 1(1) or (2) LPA 1925 and is therefore equitable (s 1(3) LPA 1925)
Easement for life		It does not appear in s 1(1) or (2) LPA 1925 and is therefore equitable (s 1(3) LPA 1925)
Lease for five years	A legal estate in s 1(1)(b) LPA 1925	
Beneficial interest under a trust		It does not appear in s 1(1) or (2) LPA 1925 and is therefore equitable (s 1(3) LPA 1925)

(*continued*)

(*continued*)

Interest	Capable of being legal	Equitable by nature
Contract to grant a legal easement		It does not appear in s 1(1) or (2) LPA 1925 and is therefore equitable (s 1(3) LPA 1925)

1.10 Formalities

There are formalities for the creation or transfer of a legal estate or interest and for the creation of an equitable interest. There are exceptions to the rules. You need to learn both the rules and the exceptions.

1.10.1 Creation or transfer of a legal estate or interest

Section 52(1) LPA 1925 provides that a deed is required to create or transfer a legal estate or interest in land. This means that the estates and interests appearing respectively in s 1(1) and 1(2) LPA 1925 must be created by deed in order to be legal.

The requirements for a deed are set out in s 1 of the Law of Property (Miscellaneous Provisions) Act 1989 (LPMPA 1989) which are that it must be:

- in writing;
- clear on its face that it is a deed;
- signed;
- witnessed (by one witness); and
- delivered.

Exceptions to the rule

Certain short-term leases require no formalities for creation. These are called parol leases and can be created orally. In order to be legal, such leases must meet the criteria set out in s 54(2) LPA 1925 as follows:

(a) The lease must be for three years or less. This would include periodic leases where the period of the lease is for three years or less. For example, a monthly periodic lease.

(b) The lease must take effect in possession. This means that the tenant must have the immediate right to possess and enjoy the land.

(c) The tenant must pay the best rent which can be reasonably obtained. This means market rent.

(d) The landlord must not charge a fine or premium. This is a one-off capital sum. For example, granting the lease for £5,000. This premium could be paid instead of rent, or in addition to it.

Usually, the creation of a legal easement requires the formality of a deed; however, certain easements (as a consequence of their method of creation) do not require this formality. This will be considered in more detail in **Chapter 3**.

1.10.2 Contract for the creation or transfer of rights in land

Many property transactions will be in two distinct stages:

Stage 1 Investigation of title leading up to exchange of contracts; and

Stage 2 Completion when the legal estate is created or transferred (subject to the relevant formalities here)

All contracts for the creation or transfer of rights in land must comply with s 2 LPMPA 1989 in order to be valid. The contract must:

- be in writing;
- incorporate all the expressly agreed terms in one document (or where contracts are exchanged in each document); and
- be signed by or on behalf of all parties.

The following transactions are examples of where the contract would need to comply with the requirements of s 2 LPMPA 1989 in order to be valid:

- the sale of a freehold or lease;
- the grant of a lease;
- the creation of an option;
- the creation of an easement.

Any variation to a contract must also comply with the requirements of s 2 LPMPA 1989.

Once contracts are exchanged, the buyer has an equitable interest in the land (an estate contract).

1.10.3 Creation or transfer of an equitable right in land

Equitable property rights can be created in a number of different ways, the most significant of which are as follows:

(a) By grant of an estate or interest which can only exist in equity;

(b) By grant of an estate or interest by a person who owns only an equitable right;

(c) By contract to create or transfer a legal estate or interest;

(d) By trying to grant a legal estate or interest but failing to use a valid deed; and

(e) By express trust.

By grant of an estate or interest which can only exist in equity

Certain equitable rights have no legal equivalents, for example a restrictive covenant. Even if these interests are created by deed, they will only ever be equitable. They are not listed in s 1(1) or (2) LPA 1925 so they are not capable of being legal – s 1(3) LPA 1925.

This type of equitable right must be created by signed written document (s 53(1) LPA 1925).

By grant of an estate or interest by a person who owns only an equitable right

A person cannot grant a greater interest than they possess. The owner of an equitable interest in land cannot grant a legal interest. For example, a person holding an equitable lease can only sell an equitable lease, not a legal lease.

This type of equitable right must be created by signed written document (s 53(1) LPA 1925).

By contract to create or transfer a legal estate or interest

A valid contract, complying with s 2 LPMPA 1989 is required. In addition, the remedy of specific performance of the contract must also be available.

Specific performance is an equitable remedy, therefore the courts will only grant it if the person seeking it has behaved justly and fairly. This is based on the equitable maxim: 'He who seeks equity must do so with clean hands.' This means that the person seeking the remedy must not be in breach of the terms of the contract.

For equity to recognise the arrangement there must be:

- a contract;
- complying with s 2 LPMPA 1989; and
- clean hands.

This is known as the doctrine in *Walsh v Lonsdale* (1882) 21 Ch D 9. The parties had made a valid contract for a seven-year lease and the tenant had taken possession of the property. The parties omitted to execute a deed in order to create a legal lease. The court recognised an equitable lease based on the existence of the contract and the availability of specific performance. The decision was based on the equitable maxim of 'equity regards as done that which ought to be done'.

In *Coatsworth v Johnson* [1886–90] All ER Rep 547 there was a valid contract for a lease of a farm but the lease was not completed by deed and therefore could not be legal. Coatsworth took possession of the farm but breached a term of the contract. The court would not recognise the equitable lease as a consequence of Coatsworth breaching the terms of the contract and therefore not having clean hands.

So a contract to create or transfer a legal property right will create an equivalent equitable property right (as long as the claimant has clean hands). For example:

- a contract to create a legal lease will create an equitable lease;
- a contract to create a legal easement will create an equitable easement.

However, a contract to transfer an existing legal estate (freehold or a lease) will create an equitable right known as an estate contract (see **Glossary**).

By trying to grant a legal estate or interest but failing to use a valid deed

In this instance, the parties do not deliberately enter a contract. They fail to use a valid deed and the court finds a contract so that the transaction does not fail entirely. For this type of equitable property rights to arise there must be:

- a contract;
- complying with s 2 LPMPA 1989; and
- clean hands.

In *Parker v Taswell* (1858) 119 ER 230 the parties had intended to grant a legal lease but the document had not been executed correctly and was not a deed. It therefore could not create a legal lease. The document satisfied the requirements for a contract and specific performance was available, therefore the document created an equitable lease.

By express trust

An express trust must be created by signed written document (s 53(1) LPA 1925).

Often an express trust is created by deed even though this level of formality is not necessary.

Exception to the rule

Implied trusts do not need to be created in writing or signed. They arise without any formality, simply as a result of the conduct of the parties (s 53(2) LPA 1925).

1.11 Approach

Take a step-by-step approach to unpacking a fact pattern to reach an answer. Do not assume that the existence of a deed means that a legal interest has been created. Always start with a basic analysis of the interest:

Step 1 – identify the interest

What hints do the facts provide as to the type of interest involved? The following may be helpful:

- Exclusive use for a fixed period = a lease.
- The right to use another landowner's land (but not creating exclusive possession) = an easement.
- An obligation not to do something on the land = a restrictive covenant.

Step 2 – is the interest capable of being legal, or is it equitable by nature?

Estates and interests which are capable of being legal appear in s 1(1) and (2) LPA 1925. If the interest does not appear in either sub-section then it is not capable of being legal. It is equitable by nature (s 1(3) LPA 1925).

Remember, an easement or profit must be created either forever or for a fixed duration to be capable of being legal (s 1(2)(a) LPA 1925). If the easement or profit is created for an indefinite time it can only be equitable (s 2(3) LPA 1925).

Step 3 – have the correct formalities been used?

If the interest is capable of being legal then a deed is required (s 52(1) LPA 1925), unless an exception applies. Check the facts carefully to ensure that a deed has been created (s 1 LPMPA 1989). If so, this creates a legal estate or interest.

If not, consider whether an exception may apply. Is the interest a short-term lease?

If the interest is equitable by nature, the relevant formalities must be complied with unless the interest is an implied trust.

Step 4 – the interest is capable of being legal, but there is no deed

Equity may intervene to recognise the interest if there is:

- a contract;
- complying with s 2 LPMPA 1989; and
- capable of being specifically performed. He who seeks equity must do so with clean hands.

Step 5 – legal, equitable or statutory?

By following steps 1 to 4 you can identify whether the interest is capable of being legal and whether it has been created validly. If it is only capable of being equitable it will only be valid if it satisfies the appropriate rules.

Home rights do not create an interest in land and require no formalities for creation.

If the formality rules have not been complied with and equity would not intervene, there would be no valid interest in land. The person claiming the right would have a licence only.

Example 1.8

Last year, Lionel (the freehold owner) granted exclusive possession by deed of 43 Tennyson Avenue ('the Property') to Amber for a period of five years. Within the deed

Amber promised to use the property only for her hairdressing business. Amber has checked the deed and discovered that Lionel's signature was not witnessed. Lionel has discovered that Amber is now using the property as a shop selling children's clothes.

What is Amber's interest? Is it legal, equitable or statutory?

Step 1 – identify the interest

The facts state that Amber has exclusive possession for a fixed duration. This has the characteristics of a lease.

Step 2 – is the interest capable of being legal, or is it equitable by nature?

The interest is capable of being legal as it appears in s 1(1)(b) LPA 1925, a term of years absolute.

Step 3 – have the correct formalities been used?

In order to be legal a lease must be created by deed – s 52(1) LPA 1925.

A deed must comply with the criteria in s 1 LPMPA 1989. The facts state that Lionel's signature was not witnessed. The document is therefore not a deed.

Step 4 – the interest is capable of being legal, but there is no deed

A lease is capable of being legal but the deed is not valid. Equity may intervene if there is:

- a contract;
- which complies with s 2 LPMPA 1989; and
- is capable of being specifically performed. He who seeks equity must do so with clean hands.

The document has been signed and is likely to contain all the expressly agreed terms (*Parker v Taswell*). However, Amber is in breach of the terms of the contract as she is using the property for something other than a hairdressing business. Amber does not have clean hands – *Coatsworth v Johnson*.

As equity would not intervene to recognise an equitable lease, Amber holds a licence only. Amber does not have an interest in land.

The parol lease exception does not apply as the lease is for more than three years.

Summary

- The definition of land is broad and includes fixtures.
- The key tests need to be applied to distinguish a fixture from a chattel (the degree and purpose of annexation).
- Only certain interests in land are capable of being legal – see s 1(1) and (2) LPA 1925.
- All interests in land can exist in equity – s 1(3) LPA 1925.
- Legal and equitable interests in land require formalities for creation (unless an exception applies).
- Neither licences nor home rights create an interest in land.
- Estates (s 1(1) LPA 1925) and interests (legal and equitable) can be divided into:

'Ownership' of the land	Owned by someone else (third party)
Fee simple absolute in possession (freehold)	Lease
Term of years absolute (leasehold)	Mortgage
	Restrictive covenant
	Easement
	Profits
	Beneficial interest under a trust (express or implied)
	Estate contact
	Option

Sample questions

Question 1

A client has entered into a contract to sell their house. After exchange of contracts, the client seeks advice about whether they may keep the freestanding oven that slots in between two of the kitchen cabinets. The oven was purchased by the client's late husband. The oven is not mentioned in the contract.

May the client remove the oven before completion?

A No, because the oven is likely to be a fixture due to the high degree of attachment.

B Yes, because the oven is likely to be a chattel due to the slight degree of attachment.

C Yes, because any item with sentimental value is always removable.

D No, because removal of the oven would cause the room to be unfit for use as a kitchen.

E No, because any item within a property is permanently part of the land and must not be removed.

Answer

The correct option is B.

The oven is freestanding and connected to the land only by its own weight and an electrical flex. The oven is likely to be a standard measurement and easy to remove and replace and therefore retains its character as a chattel.

The degree of annexation is slight and therefore options A and E are wrong. Whether an item is a fixture or chattel is determined by the two-stage test and not any sentimental value. Option C is therefore wrong.

Option D is wrong as a freestanding oven can be easily removed and replaced and does not form part of an overall architectural design.

Question 2

Last year a land owner sold part of their land to a buyer. In the conveyance (by deed) the land owner granted the buyer a right of way over the land owner's retained land for the rest of the buyer's life.

Which of the following best describes the interest that the buyer holds?

A A legal easement

B A legal lease

C A legal restrictive covenant

D An equitable easement

E An equitable lease

Answer

The correct option is D.

The interest is an easement as the facts state that the land owner granted a right of way. This has the characteristics of an easement. It is not a lease as no exclusive possession is granted. Options B and E are therefore wrong.

An easement is capable of being a legal interest but must comply with the criteria in s 1(2)(a) LPA 1925. This means that the easement must be granted for a period equivalent to a fee simple absolute in possession (freehold) or a term of years absolute (lease). The easement must be granted forever or for a fixed duration. The easement has been granted for the buyer's life and therefore does not meet this criteria. Option A is therefore wrong.

The easement can only be equitable. It is irrelevant that it has been created by a deed.

There is nothing in the facts to suggest that a restrictive covenant has been created and a restrictive covenant is not capable of being a legal interest. Option C is therefore wrong.

Question 3

A freehold land owner grants a tenant a lease for a term of two years at market rent. Nothing was recorded in writing and no fine/premium was paid.

Has a legal lease has been created?

A No, because a deed is required to create a legal lease.

B Yes, because a two-year lease is always capable of being legal.

C No, but equity may intervene and recognise an equitable lease.

D No, because no fine or premium can be paid for a parol lease.

E Yes, because the lease complies with the parol lease exception.

Answer

The correct option is E.

A lease is capable of being legal. In order to be a legal lease a deed is required. However, certain leases for three years or less do not require a deed and can be created informally provided they fall into the parol lease exception. Option A is therefore wrong in relation to the facts.

The facts state that no fine or premium was paid. Option D is therefore wrong.

Option C is wrong as the lease is a legal lease and, in any event, if it were not, equity would not intervene as there is no written contract.

Option B correctly states that some leases for a term of three years or less can be created orally, but this is not the best answer as it does not take account of the formalities required to create a legal parol lease.

2 Co-ownership and Trusts

SQE1 syllabus

- Differences between joint tenants and tenants in common in law and in equity
- Rule of survivorship
- Severance of joint tenancies
- Solving disagreements between co-owners by reference to ss 14 and 15 of the Trusts of Land and Appointment of Trustees Act (TLATA) 1996

Note that for SQE1, candidates are not usually required to recall specific case names or cite statutory or regulatory authorities. Cases are provided for illustrative purposes only.

Learning outcomes

By the end of this chapter you will be able to apply relevant core legal principles and rules appropriately and effectively, at the level of a competent newly qualified solicitor in practice, to realistic client-based and ethical problems and situations in the following areas:

- Identify the differences between legal and beneficial ownership of land
- Explain the two forms of co-ownership
- Identify the situations in which severance of a joint tenancy in equity may occur
- Explain when implied trusts may arise
- Understand how disputes are resolved under ss 14 and 15 of TLATA 1996.

2.1 Introduction

This chapter deals with the following:

- What happens when more than one person purchases land (**2.1**)
- The difference between a joint tenancy and tenancy in common in equity (**2.2**)
- How a joint tenancy in equity may be severed (**2.3**)
- Trusts of land (**2.4**)
- Settling disputes in relation to co-owned land (**2.5**)

2.1.1 What is co-ownership?

Co-ownership is where more than one person owns land at the same time (ie concurrently). It is extremely common as most couples (whether or not married) will be joint owners of land (whether freehold or leasehold).

Where there is concurrent sharing, s 1 of TLATA 1996 creates a trust of land. A trust of land will arise in the following situations:

- a landowner intentionally sets up a trust of their land by transferring title to the land to trustees for the benefit of others (an *express* trust following the formalities in s 53 LPA 1925);
- a person acquires an interest in land owned by another due to their conduct (an *implied* trust - see **2.4**); or
- land is acquired by more than one owner jointly (co-ownership).

Terminology

Trustees	These are the legal owners. Their function is an administrative one. Trustees have no entitlement to the benefit of the property. They are not entitled to live at the property or take rent from it.
Beneficiaries	These are the equitable owners. The beneficiaries are entitled to occupy the property or receive rent from it.

The trustees and the beneficiaries may be the same, or different, people. In simple terms, when the property is sold:

- the trustees must execute the deed to transfer the legal title; and
- the beneficiaries are entitled to receive the proceeds of sale.

Hence, the trustees' functions are administrative in nature and the true value of the property rests with the beneficiaries.

Example 2.1

George and Heather jointly purchase 59 Marsh Lane ('the Property'). They hold the Property as trustees for themselves as beneficiaries. They, therefore, hold the legal estate as trustees and the equitable interest as beneficiaries.

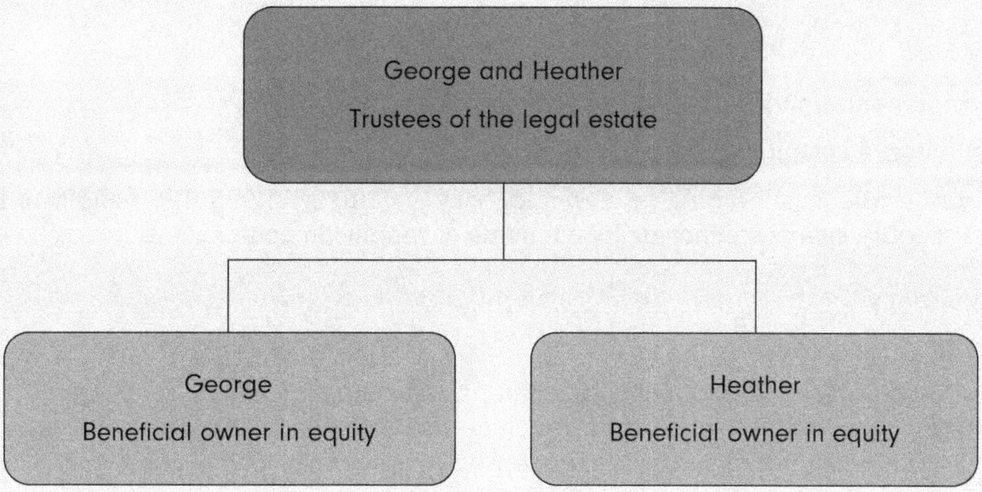

2.1.2 The legal estate

A legal estate is incapable of 'subsisting or of being created in an undivided share' – s 1(6) LPA 1925. This means that:

- the legal estate *must* be held as a joint tenancy; and
- the joint tenancy (relating to the legal estate) cannot be severed.

The trustees, therefore, hold the legal estate as joint tenants.

2.1.3 Who can be a trustee of land?

Only a person over the age of 18 can act as a trustee – s 1(6) LPA 1925. Any attempt to convey a legal estate to a minor operates as a declaration of trust that the land is held in trust for the minor – TLATA 1996, Sch 1, para 1(1).

If land is conveyed to a minor and an adult, the land is vested in the adult in trust for the minor – TLATA 1996, Sch 1, para 1(2).

2.1.4 Maximum/minimum number of trustees

The Trustee Act 1925, s 34(2) permits a maximum of four trustees. Where property is conveyed to more than four people, the first four named adults will be the trustees.

There is no minimum number of trustees. It is usual to have two trustees to ensure that the mechanism of overreaching can work (see **7.3.5**, **8.7** and **9.2.1**).

2.1.5 Powers of the trustees

Section 6(1) TLATA 1996 – trustees have all the powers of an absolute owner. This includes the power to sell or mortgage the trust land, or purchase land for the occupation of a beneficiary.

Section 11 TLATA 1996 – the trustees' powers are limited by their duty to consult the beneficiaries. The duty applies only to beneficiaries of full age and who have an interest in possession (entitled to an immediate interest in the land).

The trustees must comply (as far as is consistent with the general interests of the trust) with the wishes of the beneficiaries or (in the case of a dispute) with the majority of them (according to the value of their combined interests). The duty to consult is only in so far as it is practicable to do so.

2.2 Two forms of co-ownership

These are:

- joint tenancy; and
- tenancy in common.

The legal estate must be held as a joint tenancy – s 1(6) LPA 1925. The beneficiaries can hold their equitable interests either as joint tenants or tenants in common.

2.2.1 Joint tenancy

The right of survivorship

On the death of a joint tenant, their interest passes automatically and immediately to the surviving joint tenant(s). It does not pass under the deceased's will or intestacy. The remaining joint tenant(s) are said to survive the deceased joint tenant.

The number of joint tenants will reduce over time when they die.

Undifferentiated ownership

Joint tenants are jointly entitled to the whole of the property, and the term 'shares' is never used in the context of a joint tenancy. A joint tenant cannot point to a particular 'share' or interest in the property as their interest is in the whole.

It is possible for joint tenants to sever a joint tenancy in equity and convert the beneficial interests into a tenancy in common.

It is *not* possible to sever the joint tenancy of the legal estate. This cannot be severed to create a tenancy in common – s 36(2) LPA 1925.

Severance only ever relates to the joint tenancy in equity.

2.2.2 Tenancy in common

No right of survivorship

When a tenant in common dies their share in the property will pass to their estate in accordance with the terms of their will or the rules of intestacy. It is, therefore, possible that:

- the number of beneficial tenants in common will increase; and
- their shares can be unequal in size.

Undivided shares

Each owner is regarded as having a distinct share in the land, although the land in question has not been physically divided up between the owners. The distinct share can be equal or unequal. A tenant in common can point to a particular share in the land, for example, 'my half'.

2.2.3 Is it a joint tenancy or a tenancy in common in equity?

To find out whether the equitable interest in a property is held as joint tenants or tenants in common, we have to apply a number of tests. We shall now look at the first test:

The first test: are all four unities present?

The presence of the four unities indicates the presence of a joint tenancy in equity:

- **Unity of possession** – each co-owner has the *right* to possession of all of the land. Actual possession is not required. Unity of possession is required for *both* a joint tenancy and a tenancy in common in equity.
- **Unity of interest** – each co-owner must have identical rights over the land. This is the hallmark of a joint tenancy. A tenancy in common can have unequal shares and, therefore, no unity of interest.

- **Unity of title** – each co-owner must have acquired their interest from the same document. For example, the same transfer or conveyance.
- **Unity of time** – the co-owners receive their interests at the same time.

The absence of the unity of interest, title or time may indicate a tenancy in common. If all four unities are present, the equitable interest could be held as either a joint tenancy or a tenancy in common. So, we go on to consider the second test.

<u>The second test: does the deed transferring the land to the co-owners contain an express declaration?</u>

An express declaration of trust (complying with the formalities in s 53(1) LPA 1925) is conclusive (*Goodman v Gallant* [1986] 2 WLR 236). The document of transfer sets out how the property is to be held (regardless of the size of contribution made by any of the co-owners). Such a trust may be expressed in a set of facts as:

> 'Transferred into their joint names as express beneficial joint tenants in equity'
>
> 'Conveyed to them as express beneficial joint tenants in equity'
>
> 'The transfer contained a declaration that all four owners were beneficial joint tenants'

All three statements mean that the property has been transferred to the co-owners as joint tenants in equity. An express declaration of trust is now strongly encouraged by Land Registry.

Example 2.2

> *Mohammed and Fatima purchase 44 Lonsdale Lane ('the Property') for £280,000. Mohammed contributes £40,000 and Fatima the balance of £240,000. The transfer to Mohammed and Fatima contains a declaration that they are beneficial joint tenants.*

How do Mohammed and Fatima hold the Property?

Comment

The legal estate is held by them as trustees as joint tenants – s 1(6) LPA 1925.

The equitable interest is held as joint tenants in equity as the declaration of trust is conclusive, notwithstanding their unequal contributions.

In the absence of an express declaration, we go on to consider the third test.

<u>The third test: does the deed transferring the land to the co-owners contain words of severance?</u>

By words of severance – this means any words in the document of transfer that indicate that the co-owners are to have distinct shares. For example:

> 'I grant Greenacre to my children to be divided equally between them.'
>
> 'To A and B in equal shares.'
>
> 'Between A and B.'
>
> 'Half to A and half to B.'

Where the conveyance or transfer does not contain an express declaration or words of severance, we need to apply the fourth and last test.

<u>The fourth test: does equity presume a tenancy in common?</u>

There is a presumption that the co-owners will be joint tenants in equity on the basis that equity follows the law – *Stack v Dowden* [2007] 2 AC 432 (HL). The legal estate is always held as a joint tenancy and it is, therefore, presumed that the equitable interest will also be a joint tenancy. This presumption can be rebutted as follows:

- When the property is acquired for business use – usually a person of business would want their interest to go to their estate on their death rather than to their business partners.

- Unequal contributions to the purchase price – equity presumes a tenancy in common. The size of each tenant in common's share is in proportion to their contribution. However, in the case of a trust of the home, comments in *Stack v Dowden* suggest that the presumption for a joint tenancy in equity would apply even where there were unequal contributions.
- Post-acquisition money management – in relation to a trust of the home, there is a strong presumption in favour of a joint tenancy in equity. This can be rebutted in exceptional circumstances where it can be shown that one co-owner has provided the far greater share of the finance for the home, for example in paying all of the mortgage payments and the majority of the outgoings (*Stack v Dowden*; see **2.3.2**).

In the absence of any of these presumptions, the equitable interest will be held as joint tenants, as 'equity follows the law', ie mirrors the legal estate.

Example 2.3

Nikki, Tasha, James, Claire, Randall and Sorcha purchase 31 St James Road ('the Property') to live in while they are at University. They make an equal contribution towards the purchase price. At the time of the purchase, Nikki is 17 years old.

How is the Property held?

Legal estate

The trustees will be the first four named of full age. Nikki is 17 and, therefore, cannot be a trustee. The trustees are therefore Tasha, James, Claire and Randall. They hold the legal estate as joint tenants.

Equitable interest

Nikki, Tasha, James, Claire, Randall and Sorcha are all beneficiaries. There is no evidence of an express declaration. The four unities appear to be present and there is nothing to rebut the presumption of a joint tenancy (there were equal contributions, no words of severance and no business use). The equitable interest is, therefore, held as a joint tenancy.

The key differences between a joint tenancy and a tenancy in common are set out in the table below.

JOINT TENANCY	TENANCY IN COMMON
Each owner has an interest in the whole and owns nothing individually	Each owner has an undivided share, eg one half
The four unities must be present (possession, title, time and interest)	Only unity of possession is required but presence of four unities does not preclude a tenancy in common
The right of survivorship applies	No right of survivorship
Dealing with a 'share' will operate as severance of the joint tenancy (ie sale or mortgage)	Each owner can deal with their share separately (eg mortgage or sell)
General presumption in favour of a joint tenancy in equity on the basis that equity follows the law	A tenancy in common will arise where: • Expressly declared • Presumed on acquisition (eg business property) • Subsequent acts of severance

2.3 Severance of a joint tenancy in equity

Severance is the method by which a joint tenancy in *equity* can be converted into a tenancy in common. Severance only applies to the equitable interests. It is not possible to sever the joint tenancy of the legal estate.

Severance must be inter vivos, ie during the lifetime of the co-owner. A will cannot effect severance (*Carr v Isard* [2006] EWHC 2095 (Ch)). Although a will is written in the lifetime of the testator, it only takes effect on death.

Severance can be effected by:

- formal severance by written notice (see **2.3.1**); and
- informal severance (see **2.3.2**).

2.3.1 Written notice

A joint tenant can sever their 'share' of the joint tenancy by giving written notice to the other co-owners stating their intention to sever, either expressly or impliedly. There is no specified form for the notice and it does not need to be signed – s 36(2) LPA 1925.

Giving written notice is a unilateral act and does not require the consent of the other joint tenants.

For severance to be effective the notice must:

(a) Use appropriate wording. This must express a desire to end the joint tenancy *immediately*. Expressing a future intent or desire is insufficient – *Harris v Goddard* [1983] 1 WLR 1203; and

(b) Be received by all the other joint tenants or be deemed to have been received. Notice can be handed to the intended recipient or posted.

<u>Postal rules</u>

If posted, reliance can be placed on the deeming provisions of s 196 LPA 1925. This provision does not dictate methods of service, it is a method of proving service of notices. The relevant subsection depends on the method used.

Registered post – s 196(4)

If the notice is sent by registered or recorded letter, it is deemed to be sufficiently served if the letter is not returned (via the post office) undelivered. So, if a joint tenant chooses to send the notice via recorded letter, they can rely on the presumption set out in s 196(4) LPA 1925.

In *Re 88 Berkeley Road* [1971] 1 All ER 254 one joint tenant (X) sent notice of severance to the other joint tenant (Y) via recorded delivery. X received and signed for the letter (in order to prove notice) and died soon afterwards. Y, the recipient of the letter, stated that they had never seen the letter.

The severance was effective as the letter had not been returned undelivered and was, therefore, deemed to have been sufficiently served.

Ordinary post – s 196(3)

Any notice is sufficiently served if it is left at the last known place of abode or business in the UK of the person to be served.

In *Kinch v Bullard* [1998] 4 All ER 650 the property was owned by a married couple as joint tenants in law and equity. The wife sent notice of severance via ordinary post. The postman put the letter through the letter box. The wife subsequently picked up the letter and destroyed it as she had changed her mind about severance. The husband died shortly afterwards.

If severance had occurred, then the property would be held as tenants in common. This would mean that the deceased husband's interest would go to his estate.

If severance had not occurred, then the property would be held as a joint tenancy. This would mean that when the husband died, the rule of survivorship would apply and the wife would survive him and become the sole owner of the property.

The court found that the severance was effective as the letter had been left at the last known place of abode of the husband, even though it was not received by the intended recipient. In this case, the deeming provision in s 196(4) could not be relied upon (as the letter was sent by ordinary post) and the evidence of the postman was required in court to prove that he had placed the letter in the letter box.

Example 2.4

Martin and his husband, Jeff, purchased 33 Maple Grove ('the Property') as joint tenants in law and in equity. Martin has recently discovered that Jeff has been having an affair with Martin's best friend. Martin writes to Jeff to say that he wants the Property to be sold in a year's time and the proceeds split between them. He sends the letter by recorded post. Martin signs for the letter and then throws the letter away having reconciled with Jeff and changed his mind about severing the joint tenancy.

How do Martin and Jeff hold the Property?

Legal estate

Martin and Jeff hold the legal estate as joint tenants. This cannot be severed.

Equitable interests

Initially, Martin and Jeff hold the Property as joint tenants. Martin has attempted to sever the joint tenancy by sending a formal notice. Although his notice would be deemed to be received (as it has not been returned undelivered under s 196(4)), it lacks the necessary immediacy (Martin wants the Property sold in a year's time not immediately). Therefore, formal severance has not occurred and Martin and Jeff continue to hold the Property as joint tenants in equity.

2.3.2 Informal severance

Methods of severance were identified in *Williams v Hensman* (1861) l John & H 546:

- Acts operating on the joint tenant's share (alienation)
- Mutual agreement
- Course of dealing

In addition, severance can be effected by:

- bankruptcy;
- homicide; and
- post-acquisition money management.

Dealing with each in turn:

<u>Acts operating on the joint tenant's share (alienation)</u>

This is a unilateral act. It is when a joint tenant in equity disposes of their equitable interest by sale, gift, lease or mortgage. The disposition relates to an equitable interest and must, therefore, follow the rules in s 53(1) LPA 1925 (ie in writing and signed). Such a disposition would mean that the four unities are no longer present as between the joint tenants.

A contract to dispose of the equitable interest will also sever the joint tenancy in equity provided it complies with the requirements in s 2 LPMPA 1989 and is capable of being specifically enforceable (on the basis that equity regards as done that which ought to be done).

The disposition of the equitable interest can be to either a stranger or a fellow joint tenant.

Severance by mutual agreement

This requires the joint tenants to act together (either expressly or by implication) to sever the joint tenancy in equity or where the parties agree to deal with the land in a certain way and that method of dealing would have the effect of severing.

An oral agreement will suffice and the agreement does not need to be carried through to performance. The significance of the agreement is not that it binds the parties, but that it expresses an intention to sever the joint tenancy.

Example 2.5

Elderly widowed lovers, Mr Honick and Mrs Rawnsley, purchased a house as beneficial joint tenants. It became apparent that Mrs Rawnsley would not marry Mr Honick and it was subsequently agreed that Mr Honick would purchase Mrs Rawnsley's interest for £750. Mrs Rawnsley then changed her mind and requested a payment of £1000. No further action was taken by either party and three years later Mr Honick died.

Was there a severance?

Comment

Yes, there was an agreement supported by an intention to give valuable consideration (£750) which provided an indication of a common intention to sever (notwithstanding Mrs Rawnsley's repudiation of the agreement).

These are the facts and decision from *Burgess v Rawnsley* [1975] 1 Ch 429. In that case, Lord Denning stated:

> I think there was evidence that Mr Honick and Mrs Rawnsley did come to an agreement that he would buy her share for £750. That agreement was not in writing and it was not specifically enforceable. Yet, it was sufficient to effect a severance.

Severance by mutual conduct/course of dealing

For severance by a mutual course of conduct, the joint tenants do not have to agree to do something to sever, but must show *through their conduct* (in relation to the land and each other) that they clearly regard themselves as owning distinct shares. The parties must behave in a way that shows they assume they are tenants in common over a significant period of time:

> 'It covers only acts of the parties, including, it seems to me, negotiations which, although not otherwise resulting in any agreement, indicate a common intention that the joint tenancy should be regarded as severed.' Per Sir John Pennycuick in *Burgess v Rawnsley*

> 'A course of dealing need not amount to an agreement, expressed or implied, to sever. It is sufficient if there is a course of dealing in which one party makes clear to the other that he desires that their shares should no longer be held jointly but be held in common.' Per Lord Denning in *Burgess v Rawnsley*

The comments on mutual conduct/course of dealing in *Burgess v Rawnsley* were obiter. There is no decided case law in relation to mutual conduct/course of dealing.

Severance by bankruptcy

This is a form of involuntary alienation (ie an act operating on the joint tenant's share). Any bankruptcy affecting a joint tenant has the effect of severing the joint tenancy by causing an involuntary assignment of the equitable interest to the joint tenant's trustee in bankruptcy. Once the bankruptcy is discharged, the equitable interest reverts to the co-owner who will continue to hold it as a tenant in common.

Severance by homicide

This applies where one joint tenant unlawfully kills another joint tenant. In relation to a joint tenancy, survivorship applies meaning that the survivor of the deceased joint tenant would benefit from their crime. It is, therefore, a rule of public policy to ensure that the wrongdoer does not benefit from their crime.

Post-acquisition money management

Where a family home is bought in the joint names of an unmarried couple who are both responsible for any mortgage, but there is no express declaration of their beneficial interests:

(1) The starting point is that equity follows the law and they are joint tenants in law and in equity.

(2) That presumption can be rebutted either by the parties showing that they had a different common intention at the time of the acquisition or that they later formed the common intention that their respective shares would change. The fact that the parties had contributed to the acquisition of the home in unequal shares would not normally be sufficient to rebut the presumption of a joint tenancy; however, the parties' common intentions may change over time producing an 'ambulatory constructive trust'.

(3) Their common intention is to be deduced objectively from their conduct but, if it is not possible to ascertain this by direct evidence or by inference, then their shares are to be what the court considers fair, having regard to the whole course of dealing between them in relation to the property.

(4) Each case will turn on its own facts. Financial contributions are relevant but there are many other factors which may enable the court to decide what shares were either intended or fair.

Example 2.6

Mr Stack and Ms Dowden were an unmarried couple who lived together for 19 years. Their first property was acquired in Ms Dowden's sole name and she paid the mortgage payments and other household outgoings. Mr Stack carried out extensive repairs and improvements to the property. They then sold that house and purchased a new home in joint names, but with no express declaration of trust. A sizeable contribution was made towards the purchase from Ms Dowden's building society account. Ms Dowden contributed a greater sum to the mortgage interest payments than Mr Stack and continued to pay all the household expenses. The parties maintained separate bank accounts and made separate investments throughout their relationship. Overall, there was a substantial disparity between their respective contributions to the purchase.

How was the property held?

Comment

Ms Dowden successfully argued that the presumption of a joint tenancy should be rebutted and she should be entitled to more than 50% of the value of the property. The House of Lords agreed, using a flexible and holistic approach (as outlined above), holding that the proceeds of sale be divided as to 65% to Ms Dowden and 35% to Mr Stack.

These are the key facts from *Stack v Dowden* [2007] UKHL 17. The onus of proof was on Ms Dowden to rebut the presumption in favour of a joint tenancy in equity.

2.3.3 Effect of severance

On severance, the joint tenancy in equity becomes a tenancy in common. The precise effect depends on the number of joint tenants:

- Where there are two joint tenants in equity, they both become tenants in common in equal shares.

- Where there are three or more joint tenants in equity, only the co-owner who severs their joint tenancy becomes a tenant in common. The other joint co-owners continue to hold a joint tenancy in equity of the remaining interest.
- Their 'share' of the property is proportionate to the number of joint tenants. So, if there are three joint tenants, the co-owner who severs their joint tenancy will hold one-third as a tenant in common and the remaining co-owners will continue to hold two-thirds as joint tenants.
- When severance occurs, the individual co-owners' contributions to the purchase price is irrelevant.

Bedson v Bedson [1965] 2 QB 666 and *Goodman v Gallant* [1986] Fam 106.

Example 2.7 (Two joint tenants)

Harry and Seema purchase 77 Bottle Lane ('the Property'). Seema contributed 70% of the purchase price and Harry the remaining 30%. The transfer to them contained a declaration that the Property was held legally and beneficially as joint tenants. Harry sells his interest in the property to his brother, Joseph. Subsequently, Seema is killed in a tragic road accident. Seema left all her interest in the Property to her cousin, Ambar. Ambar now wants confirmation that she holds a 70% interest in the Property.

How is the property held?

Comment

Legal estate

The legal estate was held as a joint tenancy. On Seema's death, the rule of survivorship applies and Harry becomes the sole trustee of the legal estate.

Equitable interests

Harry and Seema held the equitable interest as joint tenants. Harry's sale to Joseph was an act operating on one joint tenant's share and severs the joint tenancy in equity. Upon severance, Harry and Seema held the equitable interest as tenants in common in equal shares. Their initial contributions are irrelevant.

On Seema's death, her interest passed to Ambar. Ambar holds a 50% interest in the Property as a tenant in common. Joseph also holds a 50% interest in the Property as a tenant in common.

Example 2.8 (More than two joint tenants)

Amy, Ben, Clive, Diana and Eddie purchase 4 Station Drive ('the Property') for them to live in whilst they are studying at University. The Property is transferred to them as express beneficial joint tenants in equity. Ben is short of money and sells his interest in the Property to Fiona.

How is the Property held?

Comment

Legal estate

There can only be a maximum of four trustees. On this basis, Amy, Ben, Clive and Diana will hold the legal estate as trustees as joint tenants (as the first four named). Ben's sale relates only to his equitable interest and does not affect his position as a trustee of the legal estate. Ben, therefore, remains a trustee.

Equitable interest

There is an express declaration which is conclusive, meaning that Amy, Ben, Clive, Diana and Eddie hold the equity as joint tenants. Ben selling his equitable interest to Fiona acts as a severance. Fiona holds one-fifth of the equitable interest as a tenant in common. The remaining four-fifths will be held by Amy, Clive, Diana and Eddie as joint tenants.

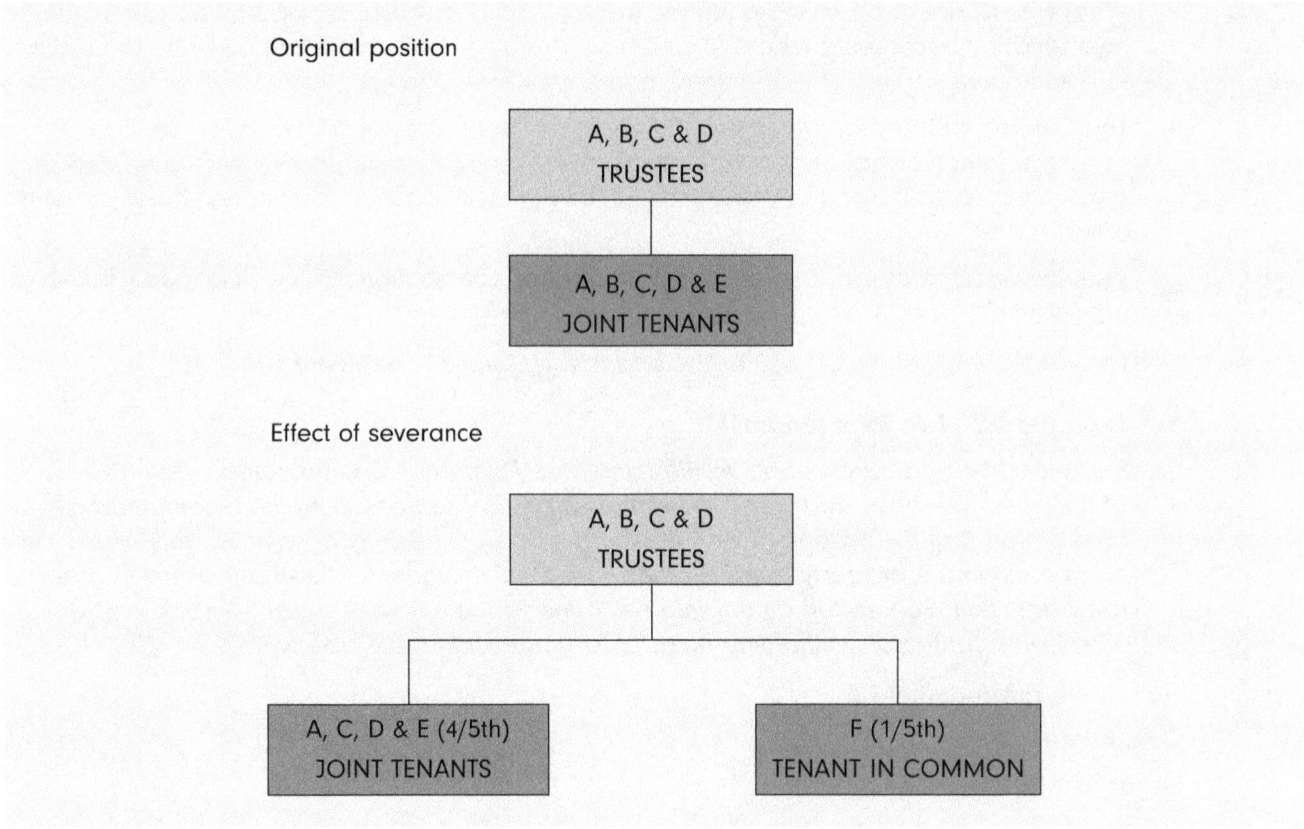

2.4 Implied trusts of land

In the absence of an express declaration of trust, a trust of land may be implied as a consequence of the conduct of the parties. This will either be a resulting or constructive trust.

<u>Resulting trust</u>

A resulting trust will arise when:

- a person, who does not hold legal title to property, makes a contribution to the purchase price of the property;
- there is no evidence that the contribution was intended as a gift or a loan; and
- the contribution must be of all or part of the purchase price at the date of acquisition (not subsequent to it).

The person then holds a beneficial interest in the property proportionate to the contribution made.

Example 2.9

Ken purchased 98 Munroe Place ('the Property') for £260,000. The Property was transferred into his sole name. Ken's friend, Barbara, paid the deposit of £26,000 and Ken paid the balance.

How is the Property held?

Comment

Legal estate

Ken holds the legal estate on trust for himself and Barbara.

Equitable interests

Barbara made a financial contribution to the purchase price on acquisition of the Property. Her interest is proportionate to her contribution, ie 10%.

Constructive trust

Lord Bridge's obiter comments in *Lloyds Bank plc v Rosset* [1991] 1 AC 107 provide a two-stage test for the creation of a constructive trust. This can be created either by:

An agreement + detrimental reliance

or

Conduct + direct financial contribution

Agreement + detrimental reliance

Lord Bridge referred to any 'agreement, arrangement or understanding' reached between the parties on how the property is to be shared beneficially. This is a question of fact and depends on the evidence of express discussions between the parties presented to the court (however imperfectly remembered or imprecise the terms of the agreement).

It is irrelevant that the agreement is based on a trick or is deceitful. For example in *Eves v Eves* [1975] 1 WLR 1338 the legal owner stated that the house could not be purchased jointly as his partner was less than 21 years of age or in *Grant v Edwards* [1986] Ch 638 where the legal owner stated that the house could not be purchased jointly as it would prejudice the divorce proceedings of his partner.

The agreement can be at the time of the purchase or subsequent to it.

The non-legal owner (asserting the benefit of the agreement) must show that they have relied upon the agreement to their detriment or significantly altered their position. The following are examples of detrimental reliance:

- Paying for improvements to the house out of their own money
- Paying all of the household bills to allow the legal owner to pay the mortgage
- Working unpaid in the legal owner's business.

The detriment must be linked to the agreement and not related to any other motive, such as love and affection.

Example 2.10

George is the sole owner of 26 Railway Cuttings ('the Property'). At the time of the purchase in 2017, George assured his girlfriend, Nicole, that the Property would be their 'forever home'. Upon the purchase of the Property, Nicole gave up her rented flat and since then has paid half of the mortgage payments for the Property.

Comment

The agreement is George's statement that the Property would be their forever home.

The detriment is that Nicole gave up her flat and paid half the mortgage payments, provided that this was in reliance of the agreement (not love and affection for George).

Nicole is a beneficiary under a constructive trust.

Conduct + direct financial contribution

In this situation, there is no evidence of an agreement or arrangement to share the property beneficially. In the absence of such an agreement, the court looks at the conduct of the parties 'both as the basis from which to infer a common intention to share the property beneficially and as the conduct relied on to give rise to a constructive trust', per Lord Bridge.

The required conduct is payment towards the purchase price initially or payment of the mortgage payments by the non-owning party. This direct financial contribution then gives rise to a common intention that the property should be shared beneficially.

Lord Bridge thought that anything less than such a direct financial contribution would be insufficient.

Example 2.11

Mr and Mrs Rosset purchased a property. The property was transferred into Mr Rosset's sole name although he promised Mrs Rosset that it would be jointly owned. The property required a complete renovation. Mrs Rosset assisted in chasing the building contractors and doing some decoration around the house. Mrs Rosset made no direct financial contributions.

Does Mrs Rosset have an interest in the property?

Comment

Following Lord Bridge's two-stage test:

- There is evidence of an agreement in that Mr Rosset promised that the property would be jointly owned. However, there was no detrimental reliance by Mrs Rosset as she had been engaged in usual family activity.
- Mrs Rosset made no direct financial contributions and, therefore, there was insufficient conduct to imply a common intention to share the property beneficially.

On this basis, Mrs Rosset had no beneficial interest in the property. This was the outcome in *Lloyds Bank plc v Rosset* [1991] 1 AC 107.

Lord Bridge's two-stage test has been criticised by Baroness Hale in obiter comments in *Stack v Dowden* [2007] 2 AC 432 where she indicated that Lord Bridge's test was too narrow and that:

> The law has indeed moved on in response to changing social and economic conditions. The search is to ascertain the parties' shared intentions, actual, inferred or imputed, with respect to the property in the light of their whole course of conduct in relation to it.

This more holistic approach was further developed in *Jones v Kernott* [2011] UKSC 53 with helpful guidance in relation to trusts of the family home where the legal estate is in one name as follows:

(a) Was it intended that the non-owning party have any beneficial interest in the property?

(b) If so, the parties' common intention must be deduced objectively from their conduct.

(c) There is no presumption of joint beneficial ownership (ie holding in equal 'shares').

(d) If there is no evidence as to what shares were intended, the court considers what is fair having regard to the whole course of dealing between them in relation to the property.

(e) Each case will turn on its own facts. Financial contributions are relevant but there are many other factors which may enable the court to decide what shares were intended or fair.

(f) Resulting trusts are not appropriate to ascertainment of beneficial interests in a family home. Constructive trusts are preferred by the courts.

The Supreme Court has not yet formally overturned the need to create a constructive trust using the two-stage test set out in *Lloyds Bank v Rosset*, save for indicating that the parties' common intention to create a trust has to be deduced objectively from their conduct. The safest approach is, therefore, to apply the two-stage test in *Lloyds Bank v Rosset* to identify whether a constructive trust has been created. If so, the more flexible approach in *Stack v Dowden* and *Jones v Kernott* can be applied to calculate the respective interests of the beneficial owners in the family home.

2.5 Settling disputes

Disputes between married couples will be resolved using legislation in relation to divorce. There is no such legislation for non-married couples and the development of case law (ie *Stack v Dowden* and *Jones v Kernott*) can be viewed as an attempt to create a framework for non-married couples.

In order for co-owned land to be sold, all the trustees need to execute the deed transferring the legal estate. When co-owners fall out and one (or more) of them wants to sell the property and the other(s) want to retain the property, such disputes can be resolved using ss 14 and 15 of TLATA 1996.

Section 14 TLATA 1996

A trustee or any person who has an interest in the property may make an application to the court for an order under s 14.

The court has wide discretion to make an order:

(a) relating to the exercise by the trustees of any of their functions; or

(b) declaring the nature or extent of the person's interest in property.

Applications under s 14 are likely to fall into one of the following categories:

- disputes regarding the size of co-ownership interests, for example where there has been no express declaration of trust
- disputes regarding the occupation of trust land
- authorising transactions without the consent of all the trustees
- disputes as to whether co-owned land should be sold.

Section 15 TLATA 1996

Section 15 of TLATA 1996 sets out the factors that the court should consider in exercising its powers under s 14. The factors in s 15(1) are:

(a) the intentions of the person or persons (if any) who created the trust;

(b) the purposes for which the property subject to the trust is held;

(c) the welfare of any minor who occupies or might reasonably be expected to occupy any land subject to the trust as his home; and

(d) the interests of any secured creditor of any beneficiary.

And

Section 15(3): '... the matters to which the court is to have regard also include the circumstances and wishes of any beneficiaries of full age and entitled to an interest in possession in property subject to the trust or (in the case of dispute) of the majority (according to the value of their combined interests).'

Subsequent case law demonstrates that the above list is not exhaustive and the court can have regard to any other relevant circumstances, although weight will always be given to a secured creditor against the needs of a child or an ill co-owner (*Bank of Ireland Home Mortgages Ltd v Bell* [2001] 2 FLR 809).

Section 15(1)(a) The intentions of the person(s) who created the trust

This is relevant where the trust has been created expressly or by will. The court will consider the settlor's intentions prior to creating the trust. The court considers the historic position.

Section 15(1)(b) The purposes for which the property subject to the trust is held

The court considers the current position. The purposes of a trust can be formulated informally and can be varied by agreement.

Where the purpose of the trust is still capable of being substantially fulfilled, particularly where the property is a family home, the court is likely to refuse and order the sale. However, where a relationship has broken down irretrievably and there are no minor children then the court is more likely to order a sale (*Jones v Challenger* [1961] 1 QB 176).

Section 15(1)(c) The welfare of any minor who occupies or might reasonably be expected to occupy any land subject to the trust as their home

In *Re Evers* [1980] 1 WLR 810, as the father had a secure home and the mother accepted responsibility for the outstanding mortgage, the court refused an order for sale. The court indicated that, if or when the circumstances changed (eg as the children grew up and left home), a renewed application by the father to sell the property would probably receive a sympathetic hearing.

Section 15(1)(d) The interests of any secured creditor of any beneficiary

Where an application is made under s 14 for sale by a trustee in bankruptcy, different considerations apply (s 335A Insolvency Act 1986).

It is now settled that the interests of the mortgagee will take priority over the interests of others in the absence of exceptional circumstances. For example, the welfare of a child aged 17 was given very little weight as against the needs of a secured creditor.

The court will also give consideration to the fact that if the property were not sold, the mortgage debt would continue to rise at the risk of wiping out the entire value of the property, or making it very difficult for the borrower to repay the debt.

Options for the court include:

1. Refuse a sale - this is likely if the purpose of acquisition can still be fulfilled.
2. Order a sale - this solution is the one normally adopted where the purposes for which the property was acquired have clearly failed, for example the property was acquired for use in a business and that business has failed.
3. Refuse a sale, but make an order regulating the right to occupy the property - for example, where a relationship has broken down as a consequence of the violence of one towards the other, a sale may be refused but the person in occupation may be ordered to pay rent to the person excluded from occupation (by their violence). This is very rare.
4. In exceptional cases, partition the co-owned property.

Example 2.12

Archie, Blake, Cherry and Duncan purchase 12 Acacia Avenue ('the Property') for them to live in whilst they complete their PgDL and SQE courses. The transfer to them expressly declared a beneficial tenancy in common in equal shares.

Blake decided early in the PgDL course that law was not for her and sold her interest to Archie. Duncan has now completed his SQE and secured a training contract with an international firm. Duncan is keen for the Property to be sold, whereas Archie and Cherry would like to remain in the property as they are planning to work for local firms.

How is the property held?

Comment

Legal estate

Archie, Blake, Cherry and Duncan hold the legal estate as trustees as joint tenants. Although Blake sold her equitable interest, she remains as a trustee.

In order for the Property to be sold, all four would need to execute the transfer document.

Equitable interest

The beneficial interest was originally held as a tenancy in common in equal shares. Blake's sale to Archie meant that the beneficial interests were held as to:

Archie ½ (his original ¼ plus the ¼ purchased from Blake)

Cherry ¼

Duncan ¼

Sections 14 and 15 TLATA 1996

Duncan has the right to apply to the court under s 14 as both a trustee and beneficiary under the trust. The court will consider the s 15 factors. The most relevant are:

> Section 15(1)(b) The purposes for which the property subject to the trust is held – Archie and Cherry could argue that the purposes of the trust are being still substantially fulfilled in providing them a home while they complete their courses and training contracts.
>
> Section 15(3) The beneficiaries are of full age and entitled to an interest in possession, and therefore, the majority according to the value of their combined interests, take precedence. On the facts, this would be Archie and Cherry who together hold ¾ of the equitable interest.

On this basis, the court would be likely to refuse a sale.

Summary

- Section 1 of TLATA 1996 automatically creates a trust of land when more than one person owns land.
- The legal estate is always held as a joint tenancy (s 1(6) LPA 1925) and the trustees have all the powers of an estate owner (s 6 TLATA 1996).
- Beneficial owners can hold their equitable interests as either joint tenants or tenants in common.
- In the absence of an express declaration (which is conclusive), if the four unities are present, there is a presumption in favour of a joint tenancy.
- That presumption can be rebutted (ie words of severance or business use).
- The right of survivorship applies to joint tenancies (but not tenancies in common).
- A joint tenancy in equity can be severed formally or informally.
- A co-owner severing a joint tenancy in equity (where there are more than two co-owners) holds as a tenant in common (in proportion to the number of co-owners) and the remaining co-owners continue to hold the remainder as joint tenants.
- A dispute between co-owners may be resolved using ss 14 and 15 of TLATA 1996.

Sample questions

Question 1

A solicitor acts for a husband and wife in the purchase of a freehold property ('the Property') for £350,000. The wife contributed £150,000 and the husband contributed the remaining £200,000. The Property is transferred to them as express beneficial joint tenants in equity.

Which of the following best describes how the Property is held?

A The Property is held as a tenancy in common due to the unequal contributions made to the purchase price.

B The Property is held legally and beneficially as joint tenants due to the express declaration of trust.

C The Property is held as a joint tenancy as the four unities are present.

D The equitable interests are held in a tenancy in common as the presumption for a joint tenancy has been rebutted by unequal contributions.

E The equitable interests are held as a joint tenancy as the express declaration of trust is conclusive.

Answer

The correct option is B.

The husband and wife hold the legal estate as trustees as joint tenants (s 1(6) LPA 1925). The four unities are present which would indicate a joint tenancy (or a tenancy in common). Option C is correct but is not the best answer as it does not reflect the express declaration.

There is an express declaration that the husband and wife hold the equitable interests as joint tenants. Option E is, therefore, correct, but not the best answer as it does not take account of how the legal estate is held.

The express declaration is conclusive, notwithstanding the unequal contributions made to the purchase price. Options A and D are, therefore, wrong.

Question 2

Four students (a chemistry student, an economics student, a geography student and a music student) purchased a property ('the Property') for them to live in whilst they studied at university. The chemist, economist and geographer each provided 20% of the purchase price. The musician contributed the remaining 40% of the purchase price. The Property was transferred to them as beneficial joint tenants in equity.

The economist struggled financially and mortgaged his interest in the Property to a bank. He subsequently received a large inheritance and managed to pay off the mortgage.

The chemist was killed in a car accident and, in her will, left her interest in the Property to her sister.

Which of the following best describes how the *equitable interests* in the Property are now held?

A The economist holds 25% as a tenant in common, with the geographer and the musician holding the remaining 75% as joint tenants.

B The economist, the geographer and the sister hold 20% each, with the musician holding 40% as tenants in common.

C The economist and the sister each hold 25% as tenants in common with the geographer and the musician holding 50% as joint tenants.

D The economist holds 20% as a tenant in common, with the geographer and the musician holding the remaining 80% as joint tenants.

E The economist holds 20% as a tenant in common with the musician and the geographer holding a joint tenancy, with the musician holding 50% and the geographer holding 30%.

Answer

The correct option is A.

Looking at the facts chronologically:

- The transfer of the Property to the co-owners contained an express declaration of trust. The equitable interests were, therefore, held as a joint tenancy at the outset, despite the unequal contributions made by the co-owners. Option A is, therefore, correct.
- When the economist mortgaged his interest, this severed the joint tenancy in relation to the economist. The effect was that the economist held a tenancy in common for 25% (being proportionate to the number of co-owners – four co-owners and, therefore, the economist is entitled to 25%). The other three students continued to hold the remaining 75% as a joint tenancy. Option D is, therefore, wrong.
- When the chemist died she was a joint tenant and the rule of survivorship applied. Her will, leaving her interest to her sister, was of no effect. The other joint tenants, the geographer and the musician, survived her. Options B and C are, therefore, wrong as the sister has no interest in the Property.
- Option E is incorrect as identifying shares is inconsistent with a joint tenancy. Plus, the maths is wrong in that the economist holds 25%.

Question 3

A father gifts his house ('the Property') to his children (a son, a step-son, a daughter and a step-daughter) as beneficial joint tenants. The Property is transferred to them. At the time of the transfer, the step-daughter is 17 years old.

The son is offered a well-paid job in Paris and sells his interest in the Property to a friend. The friend immediately moves into the Property. The son retires as a trustee.

At the step-daughter's 18th birthday party, the step-son (knowing he is terminally ill) gives the daughter and step-daughter a written notice stating that he wishes to immediately sever his joint tenancy. Subsequently, the step-son dies and, in his will, leaves his interest in the Property to his wife.

Which one of the following best describes how the Property is held?

A The trustees are the daughter and step-daughter who hold for the friend, the wife and themselves as joint tenants in equity.

B The daughter is the remaining trustee and she holds for the friend as a tenant in common as to 25% and the step-son, the daughter and the step-daughter as joint tenants of the remaining 75%.

C The daughter and step-son are the trustees holding for the friend and the wife as tenants in common (25% each) and the daughter and step-daughter as joint tenants of the remaining 50%.

D The trustee is the daughter holding for herself and the step-daughter as joint tenants of 50% and the friend and the wife as tenants in common of 25% each.

E The trustees are the daughter and step-daughter who hold for themselves and the friend and wife as tenants in common as to 25% each.

Answer

The correct option is D.

Looking at the facts chronologically:

Legal estate

The original trustees were the son, the step-son and the daughter who held the legal estate as a joint tenancy. The step-daughter could not be a trustee as she was a minor and she is not automatically appointed as a trustee when she reaches the age of 18. Therefore, options A and E are wrong. After all the events, the daughter remains the sole trustee (see below).

Equitable interests

There was an express declaration of trust and the four children held as beneficial joint tenants.

The son sells his interest

The son selling his interest to the friend severs the joint tenancy in relation to the son's equitable interest. The friend therefore holds 25% as a tenant in common (there being four joint tenants). The other children continue to hold the remaining 75% as joint tenants.

The son resigns as a trustee. This means that the remaining trustees of the legal estate are the step-son and the daughter.

The step-son's notice

This is formal severance (s 36(2) LPA 1925) and complies with the requirements as it is in writing, is given to the other joint tenants and expresses the necessary immediacy. This severs the step-son's equitable interest so that he holds 25% as a tenant in common.

Option B is, therefore, wrong as it does not take account of the severance by written notice.

The step-son's death

In relation to the legal estate, the daughter survives the step-son and becomes the sole trustee. Option C is, therefore, wrong as the step-son has died and cannot, therefore, be a trustee.

In relation to the equitable interest, the step-son had severed the joint tenancy and, at the time of his death, was a tenant in common. Survivorship does not occur and the step-son's interest goes to the wife. The equitable interests are held as follows:

The wife = 25% as a tenant in common

The friend = 25% as a tenant in common

The daughter and step-daughter = 50% as joint tenants.

3 Easements

SQE1 syllabus

- Essential characteristics of easements
- Methods for creation of easements

Note that for SQE1, candidates are not usually required to recall specific case names or cite statutory or regulatory authorities. In this chapter, however, the creation of easements by reference to the rule in Wheeldon v Burrows and s 62 LPA 1925 may be referred to in the SQE assessment as such.

Learning outcomes

By the end of this chapter you will be able to apply relevant core legal principles and rules appropriately and effectively, at the level of a competent newly qualified solicitor in practice, to realistic client-based and ethical problems and situations in the following areas:

- Understand the difference between an easement and a profit
- Identify and apply the essential characteristics of an easement
- Explain the methods by which an easement can be created.

3.1 Essential basics and formalities

An easement is a right for one landowner to make use of another parcel of land for the benefit of their own land. For example, a right of way.

A profit (or profit a prendre) is a right to go on to somebody else's land and remove from the land something which exists naturally. For example, a right to:

- catch and take fish
- graze animals
- extract minerals such as gravel or chalk
- hunt or shoot

In this chapter, the terms 'easement' and 'profit' are used interchangeably. The key differences between easements and profits are highlighted where necessary.

3.1.1 Is it capable of being legal?

Easements are capable of being legal, but only if they meet the requirements of s 1(2)(a) LPA. In order to be capable of being legal, the right must be granted for the equivalent of either:

- an estate in fee simple absolute in possession (freehold), ie forever; or
- a term of years absolute (leasehold), ie for a fixed ascertainable duration.

An easement created for an uncertain duration is, therefore, not capable of being legal and will exist in equity only - s 1(3) LPA 1925.

3.1.2 Formalities

A deed is required to create a legal easement - s 52(1) LPA 1925. The deed must meet the requirements set out in s 1 LPMPA 1989.

However, legal easements can be created without the formality of a deed - see **3.3**.

If an agreement for an easement is entered into which complies with s 2 LPMPA 1989, this creates a contract for an easement, enforceable in equity, following the doctrine in *Walsh v Lonsdale*.

3.1.3 Terminology

Servient tenement	The land over which the easement is exercised (the burdened land)
Dominant tenement	The land that enjoys the right (the benefitted land)
Servient owner	The owner of the servient tenement
Dominant owner	The owner of the dominant tenement
Grant	The land owner creates an easement in favour of the buyer
Reservation	The land owner creates an easement in favour of their own land when selling to a buyer

Example 3.1

Graham is the freehold owner of a farm called Home Farm. The farm consists of a farmhouse (where Graham lives), a barn and some farmland. Graham sells the barn to Thomas. The only means of access to the barn is via a track crossing Graham's retained farmland. Graham must grant a right of way to Thomas over the farmland.

The drains serving Graham's farmhouse run under the land forming part of the barn sold to Thomas. Graham must reserve a right to use the drains in the transfer to Thomas.

The farmland (owned by Graham) will be the servient tenement in respect of the right of way and the dominant land in relation to the drain.

The barn (owned by Thomas) will be the dominant tenement in relation to the right of way and the servient land in relation to the drain.

The right of way is a grant of an easement.

The right to use the drains is a reservation of an easement.

3.2 Is it an easement?

There is no legal definition of an easement. There is also no exhaustive list of types of easements. New types of easements can be recognised:

> 'The categories of servitude and easements must alter and expand with the changes that take place in the circumstances of mankind.' *Dyce v Lady James Hay* (1852)1 Macq 305

New types of easement are generally recognised as being analogous to existing easements. For example:

- the right to erect a satellite dish as being analogous to a right to erect a sign; and
- the right to park as being analogous to an easement for storage.

The judgement of Evershed MR in *Re Ellenborough Park* [1956] Ch 131 confirmed that four essential characteristics must be present in order for a right to exist as an easement:

1. There must be a dominant and a servient tenement.
2. The easement must accommodate the dominant tenement.
3. The dominant and servient tenements must not be both owned and occupied by the same person.
4. The easement must be capable of forming the subject matter of the grant.

1. There must be a dominant and a servient tenement

An easement can only exist if it is attached to (or appurtenant to) the dominant land. It is, therefore, essential that there is an identifiable dominant and servient tenement in existence at the time of the grant.

An easement cannot exist 'in gross'. This is where only a servient tenement is identified, without any dominant land.

The rationale for this rule is that, when an easement is created, it becomes part of the land. Remember that an easement is included in the definition of land in s 205 LPA. Any future owner of the dominant tenement enjoys the benefit of the easement. Permitting easements to be created in gross would create burdens of uncertain extent which may make land unattractive to a buyer. Ensuring that there is an identifiable dominant tenement creates greater certainty.

Any attempt to create an easement without an identifiable dominant tenement will create a licence only. However, a profit can exist in gross and only a servient tenement need be identified when creating a profit.

2. **The easement must accommodate the dominant tenement**

The right must be connected with the normal enjoyment of the dominant tenement. Whether there is such a connection is a question of fact:

> A right of way over land in Northumberland cannot accommodate land in Kent.
> *Bailey v Stephens* (1862) 12 CB (NS) 91

However, the dominant and servient tenements do not need to join each other, but they should be close enough to establish a connection between the two. In *Pugh v Savage* [1970] 2 All ER 353 the dominant and servient tenements were separated by another parcel of land. The court held that the dominant and servient tenements were sufficiently close to the easement to accommodate the dominant tenement.

In addition, the right must benefit the land itself and not just the owner in their personal capacity. The following guidelines can assist:

- Does the right improve the marketability of the land; and/or
- Would any owner of the land see it as a benefit?

The right to use a communal garden has been held to be a valid easement (*Re Ellenborough Park*). However, a right to put pleasure boats on a canal was held not to be an easement. This was on the basis that there was no connection with the ordinary use of the dominant land. The canal boat business was simply an independent business enterprise (*Hill v Tupper* (1863) 159 ER 52). This can be contrasted with a case involving a pub sign. The sign provided directions to the pub and was placed within the grounds of the property (the servient land) fronting the pub (the dominant land). The court found that the easement was connected with the manner in which the land was used as the sign was a method of communicating to the public the location of the pub and, therefore, supported the business run on the dominant land (*Moody v Steggles* (1879) 12 Ch D 261).

3. **The dominant and servient tenements must not be both owned and occupied by the same person**

As an easement is a right exercised over one piece of land for the benefit of another, you cannot have an easement over your own land. The dominant and servient owners must be different people.

This 'principle of diversity' is satisfied in relation to a landlord and tenant situation. A landlord will own the freehold interest, and grant a lease over part of the property. Here, the land is occupied by different people and, therefore, the landlord can create an easement in favour of the tenant to be exercised over the landlord's retained land (not forming part of the lease).

Rights exercised by the sole owner of two separate properties over one of them are called 'quasi-easements'. These are rights that have all the other characteristics of an easement, save for diversity of ownership/occupation. Quasi-easements can be converted to easements on a sale of part of the land (see **3.3.4**).

4. **The easement must be capable of forming the subject matter of the grant**

As a legal interest under s 1(2)(a) LPA, an easement must be capable of being granted by deed and, therefore, must be capable of precise definition.

There must be a capable grantor. This means the person who grants the right must have the power to do so. There must also be a capable grantee. For example, it would not be possible to grant rights to the inhabitants of the village, since they are a vague and fluctuating body.

Four main points have emerged from this fourth criteria:

(a) An easement must be capable of reasonably exact definition.

(b) An easement must not involve any expenditure by the servient owner.

(c) An easement must not be so extensive as to amount to a claim to joint possession of the servient tenement.

(d) The law is very cautious when it comes to a claim for a new type of negative easement.

To take each in turn:

(a) **An easement must be capable of reasonably exact definition**

An easement must be clearly defined. There can be no easement for a general flow of air to a timber drying shed. This was viewed as being 'too vague and too indefinite' (*Harris v De Pinna* (1886) 33 Ch D 238).

Similarly, there is no general right to light. An easement of light can only exist where it is sufficiently definite and the light is enjoyed via a defined aperture, eg a window (*Colls v Home and Colonial Stores* [1904] AC 179). In addition, the person claiming the right to light must demonstrate an infringement as follows:

> The light reaching the windows [of the dominant building] must be sufficient according to the usual notions of mankind for the comfortable enjoyment of the building, bearing in mind the type of building and its locality.

It is not possible for a right to a view to be an easement on the basis that 'the law does not give an action for such things of delight' (*William Aldred's Case* [1610] 9 Co Rep 57b).

There has been some debate as to whether a right to use the land for recreational purposes can be an easement. This was accepted in *Re Ellenborough Park* on the basis that the use of a communal garden was analogous to the use of a garden attached to a house. The issue appears to be settled by the Supreme Court judgement in *Regency Villas Title Ltd v Diamond Resorts (Europe) Ltd* [2018] UKSC 57 where the court held that easements could exist in relation to a golf course, swimming pool or tennis court on the basis that:

> Whatever may have been the attitude in the past to 'mere recreation or amusement', recreation and sporting activity of the type exemplified by the facilities at Broome Park is so clearly a beneficial part of modern life that the common law should support structures which promote and encourage it, rather than treat it as devoid of practical utility or benefit.

The court emphasised that the easement must have all the essential characteristics set out in *Re Ellenborough Park*. As the use of the dominant land was itself recreational, being a timeshare property, the condition that the easement must accommodate the dominant tenement was satisfied.

(b) **An easement must not involve any expenditure by the servient owner**

'It is an essential feature of an easement that it merely requires the owner of the servient tenement to suffer something to be done on the servient tenement: a positive obligation on the owner of the servient tenements to do something is inconsistent with the existence of such an easement' (*Rance v Elvin* (1985) 49 P & CR 65).

For example, where a landowner grants a right of way over their land for the benefit of some adjoining land, there is no implied obligation on the landowner to maintain the right of way. However, the owner of the dominant tenement has the right to carry out repair works.

In relation to the right of support, the servient owner cannot deliberately withdraw support.

There is one, rather odd, exception in relation to an easement of fencing from Lord Denning's decision in *Crow v Wood* [1971] 1 QB 77. This was seen as a 'spurious kind of easement' which amounts to a right to require the owner of adjoining land to keep the boundary fence in repair. The principal appears to be limited to a rural setting where it is of great importance to maintain stock proof fences (ie fences that are capable of restraining farm animals who might otherwise damage themselves or surrounding crops).

(c) **An easement must not be so extensive as to amount to a claim to joint possession of the servient tenement**

An easement cannot give exclusive, joint or substantially permanent possession of the servient tenement. In other words the right claimed must not be too extensive. It must not be so extensive as to exclude the grantor completely from possession of the servient tenement.

This is judged both:

- temporally - the amount of time taken; and
- spatially - the amount of space used.

This causes problems for easements of storage and parking:

Wright v MacAdam [1949] 2 KB 744

The rights of the tenant to store domestic coal in a shed on the landlord's land was accepted as an easement. However, the case has been widely criticised for lacking any detailed analysis of the right of storage. It is unclear from the facts whether the tenant had exclusive use of the coal shed or, indeed, the size of the coal shed.

Grigsby v Melville [1972] 1 WLR 1355

The defendant claimed the right to store articles in a cellar beneath the neighbouring owner's living room floor. The claim failed as it amounted to an extensive use of a confined space. In simple terms, the defendant had filled the cellar.

The question is, therefore, one of fact and degree. The greater the intensity of the use claimed, the less likely the courts will be to recognise the existence of an easement.

Example 3.2

Mr Copeland is the owner of an orchard and adjoining house. Access to the orchard from the road is via a long narrow strip of land ('the Land'). Mr Greenhalf is a wheelwright (someone making and repairing wheels) who owns land adjoining Mr Copeland's land. Mr Greenhalf claims an easement to store and repair vehicles in connection with his business on the Land.

Is this an easement?

Comment

These are the key facts in *Copeland v Greenhalf* [1952] Ch 488 where the court found that the claim was too extensive to constitute an easement. This was because there was no limit placed on the number of vehicles that could be stored on the Land, nor on the length of time for which they could be stored. It, therefore, amounted to a claim to joint beneficial use over the Land and not an easement.

Easement of parking?

Based on the decisions outlined above, it was believed that an easement of parking would not be recognised by the courts:

London and Blenheim Estates v Ladbroke Retail Parks [1992] 1 WLR 1278

The claimant owned part of a shopping centre and claimed that the right of customers to park on a central car park was an easement. The judge (obiter dicta) accepted that there could be an easement to park vehicles on a piece of servient land provided that the servient land was sufficiently large.

The issue was, therefore, a question of degree. The right would not be an easement if the effect of it was to leave the servient owner without any reasonable use of their land.

Batchelor v Marlow [2003] 1 WLR 764

The respondents (owners of a garage business) claimed the right to park up to six cars on land belonging to the appellant between 8.30am and 6pm, Monday to Friday. Six cars would cover the whole of the servient land.

The Court of Appeal concluded that this left the appellant with 'no reasonable use of the land'. This rendered the appellant's ownership of the land illusory contrary to the underlying principles regarding easements. In these circumstances the right claimed was not capable of being an easement.

Moncrieff v Jamieson [2007] 1 WLR 260

This was a Privy Council decision where the test established in *Batchelor v Marlow* was criticised. Lord Scott expressed the view that the test needed some qualification, making the following obiter comment:

> the test [is not] whether the servient owner is left without reasonable use of his land [but] whether [he] retains possession and, ... control of the servient land.

Lord Scott noted that where rights to park were granted, the servient owner still retained the ability to build above or under the parking area, or to place advertising hoardings on the walls.

Lord Neuberger concurred with Lord Scott stating that 'a right can be an easement notwithstanding that the dominant owner effectively enjoys exclusive occupation, on the basis that the essential requirement is that the servient owner retains possession and control'.

Virdi v Chana & Others [2008] EWHC 2901 (Ch)

The judge found that despite the Privy Council (in *Moncrieff v Jamieson*) criticising the principal from *Batchelor v Marlow*, the court did not overrule it. On this basis the court (in *Virdi v Chana*) felt bound by the principal in *Batchelor v Marlow* and dismissed the claim for an easement of parking as leaving the servient owner no reasonable use of their land.

(d) **The law is very cautious when it comes to a claim for a new type of negative easement**

A positive easement is one where the benefit of the easement is enjoyed by occupants of the dominant land performing some activity. For example, a right:

- of way
- of drainage
- to erect a sign

A negative easement is where the right exercised by the dominant owner prevents the servient owner from doing something on their land. The only negative easements recognised at law are those of light, air and support.

The House of Lords in *Hunter v Canary Wharf Ltd* [1997] 2 All ER 426 considered that the claimants were not entitled to an easement of television reception. This was on the basis that it would impose an immense burden on a person wishing to build on the servient land. The decision appeared to affirm the principle that the court would not recognise any new negative easements. Negative easements are viewed with caution as they could prevent the owner of the servient land from enjoying their land to the full and would mean they would not be free to carry out legitimate development.

In English law, there is no automatic right to light. The law does not recognise any right to a general flow of light to a building, but a legal right to light can exist in relation to a defined aperture, as an easement.

Once a right to light has been established, it must then be proved that the right has been infringed. It must be demonstrated that the amount of light remaining has been reduced to a level below that which 'is required for the ordinary purposes of inhabitancy or business of the tenement according to the ordinary notions of mankind'. This includes past and future purposes, if reasonable. Ordinary purposes will depend on the actual nature of the property and how it is being used.

Example 3.3

Harrison is the freehold owner of Stoney Farm. This consists of a large farmhouse, outbuildings and farm land. Harrison grants (by deed) the right for Mary to park her large pizza van on a small area of land next to the entrance gate to Stoney Farm. Mary is the freehold owner of the land adjoining Stoney Farm, called Hazy Meadow. Mary uses the van to cook and deliver pizza as part of her business.

Is this an easement?

Comment

Using the *Re Ellenborough Park* criteria:

- There is a dominant tenement (Hazy Meadow) and a servient tenement (Stoney Farm).
- It is questionable whether the right accommodates the dominant tenement. It appears to benefit Mary's pizza delivery business and is not attached (or appurtenant) to the land.
- The dominant and servient tenements are owned/occupied by different people, with Harrison owning Stoney Farm and Mary owning Hazy Meadow.
- The right may be too extensive to be an easement. Mary parks a large van on a small area. This would leave Harrison with no reasonable enjoyment of his land.

On the basis that the right does not accommodate the dominant tenement and it is too extensive an easement has not been created, Mary simply has a licence.

3.3 Has it been created?

There are a number of methods by which an easement can be created. They are as follows:

- Express grant/reservation
- Implied by necessity
- Implied by common intention
- The rule in *Wheeldon v Burrows*
- Section 62 LPA 1925
- Prescription.

Increasingly courts tend to treat easements implied by necessity and those implied by common intention as one category.

3.3.1 Express grant/reservation

An express grant of an easement is where the servient owner executes a deed granting the dominant owner an easement over land owned by the servient owner. It is an agreement made knowingly and deliberately.

An express reservation is where the seller reserves/retains rights over the land they are selling. The land retained becomes the dominant land, and the land sold the servient land.

3.3.2 Implied by necessity

This applies to grants *and* reservations.

An easement of necessity would arise on the sale of a land-locked parcel of land. This is where the land has no means of access to it from the public highway. The circumstances in which the law is willing to imply the grant of an easement of necessity are extremely limited:

> In my opinion, an easement of necessity means an easement without which the property retained cannot be used at all, and not merely necessary to the reasonable enjoyment of the property. *Union Lighterage v London Graving Dock Company* [1902] 2 Ch 557

A claim for an easement of necessity would, therefore, be defeated if there was an alternative means of access, even if that alternative access was dangerous.

An easement of necessity can only be used for those purposes for which the dominant land was being used at the time the necessity arose, ie at the date of the grant/transfer (*London Corporation v Riggs* [1880] 13 Ch D 798).

<u>What to look for in a set of facts</u>

The land has no means of access other than the right claimed.

3.3.3 Implied by common intention

This applies to grants *and* reservations.

Where land is conveyed for a purpose known to the grantor, any easement over land retained by the grantor which is essential in order for that purpose to be carried out is implied into the grant in favour of the grantee.

Wong v Beaumont Property Trust Ltd [1965] 1 QB 173

Wong became the tenant of a lease of the ground floor of a property. The lease required the let property to be used as a restaurant and included an obligation on the tenant that no noxious smells would be emitted by the restaurant. The only way to comply with this obligation was to build a ventilation duct through the remaining part of the building owned by Beaumont Property Trust.

An easement was implied as the ventilation shaft was needed to ensure that the obligation in the lease could be complied with:

> The law will readily imply the grant or reservation of such easements as may be necessary to give effect to the common intention of the parties to grant of real property, with reference to the manner or purposes in and for which the land granted is to be used. But it is essential for this purpose that the parties should intend that the subject matter of the grant should be used in some definite and particular manner which may or may not involve this definite and particular use. That is the principle which underlies all easements of necessity. (per Lord Denning MR)

<u>What to look for in a set of facts</u>

A common purpose known to the parties. The right claimed is needed in order for the common purpose to be fulfilled.

3.3.4 The rule in *Wheeldon v Burrows*

This applies only to the grant of an easement and not a reservation. It is thought that the rule has no application to profits.

The effect of *Wheeldon v Burrows* (1869) LR 12 Ch D 1281 is to convert 'quasi-easements' into easements. This occurs when a land owner sells part of their land. Any quasi-easements exercised by the landowner will pass to the buyer subject to certain conditions being satisfied:

(a) the existence of a quasi-easement prior to the sale;

(b) the right must be continuous and apparent;

(c) the right must be necessary to the reasonable enjoyment of the land sold; and

(d) the right must be in use at the time of the sale.

(a) The existence of a quasi-easement prior to the sale

An easement can only exist if there is a dominant and servient tenement – *Re Ellenborough Park.* Rights exercised by a land owner over their own land cannot be an easement. However, such rights can be described as a quasi-easement. They have the characteristics of an easement save for the fact that there is no diversity of ownership.

(b) Continuous and apparent

This denotes some form of habitual enjoyment obvious from an inspection of the land. This must be a careful inspection by a person 'ordinarily conversant with the subject', for example, a surveyor.

In *Ward v Kirkland* [1967] Ch 194 Ungoed-Thomas J stated:

> [these words] seem to be directed to there being on the servient tenement a feature which would be seen on inspection and which is neither transitory nor intermittent, for example, drains, paths.

(c) The right must be necessary to the reasonable enjoyment of the land sold

The standard of necessity in *Wheeldon v Burrows* is less stringent than for an easement of necessity. The presence of an alternative right may not, necessarily, defeat a claim:

Wheeler v Saunders [1996] Ch 20

A right of way was claimed, although there was in existence an alternative means of access. The claim failed as the alternative access was just as convenient as the right claimed. Therefore, the right claimed could not be said to be necessary to the reasonable enjoyment of land.

Millman v Ellis (1996) 71 P & CR 158

A right of way was claimed, although (as in the above case) there was in existence an alternative means of access. The alternative route was dangerous and, therefore, the claim succeeded as the right of way claimed was necessary for the reasonable enjoyment of the land in order to avoid the dangerous route.

(d) The right must be in use at the time of the sale

The rule in *Wheeldon v Burrows* will only be effective if the quasi easement was in use at the time of the sale of the land.

Provided all of the above conditions are met, the rule in *Wheeldon v Burrows* has the effect of converting a quasi-easement into a full, legal easement.

The rule only applies in relation to the grant of easements in favour of a buyer. The rule does not assist the seller on the basis that the seller has power and control over the terms of the sale contract. The seller may, therefore, reserve whatever rights they wish.

<u>What to look for in a set of facts</u>

The land was in common ownership and the owner exercised quasi-easements over their own land. The land owner then sold part of the land.

There is no requirement for a conveyance in *Wheeldon v Burrows*. A contract, recognised in equity, will suffice.

Example 3.4

Andrew owns a large house with extensive grounds ('the Property'). Several years ago he built a cottage in the grounds ('the Cottage') which he has used to accommodate his guests. He and his guests have regularly used a track that runs across the Property in order to access the Cottage. This avoids use of a busy main road. Andrew sells the Cottage to Helen together with a right of way over the main drive. The transfer made no mention of the use of the track in the transfer document.

Would *Wheeldon v Burrows* apply?

Comment

Applying the criteria to the facts:

(a) Andrew and his guests' use of the track amounts to a quasi-easement. It has all the characteristics of an easement except a dominant and servient tenement owned or occupied by separate people.

(b) The use of the track has been continuous and apparent in that it has been used regularly and presumably the track would be visible on an inspection of the land.

(c) The right is necessary for the reasonable enjoyment of the land as it avoids a busy main road.

(d) The facts suggest that the right of way over the track may have been in use at the time of the sale to Helen.

On this basis the rule in *Wheeldon v Burrows* would apply and the Cottage would have the benefit of a legal easement over the track running over the Property.

3.3.5 Section 62 LPA 1925

Section 62 of LPA 1925 is a word-saving provision, created at a time when conveyances were handwritten. It has the effect that on a conveyance of land, if nothing to the contrary is stated in the deed, the conveyance is deemed to pass to the buyer not just the buildings and fixtures but all liberties privileges easements rights and advantages whatsoever appertaining or reputed to appertain to the land or any part thereof or at the time of the conveyance enjoyed with the land. The section operates to pass automatically to a buyer all existing rights, without the necessity of formal words in the conveyance.

Case law has had the effect of extending the scope of s 62 to create new easements:

Wright v MacAdam [1949] 2 KB 744

Mr MacAdam ('M') let a flat to Mrs Wright ('W') for one week. She continued in occupation and subsequently M gave her permission to store her coal in his coal shed.

M then granted a new tenancy to W. No reference was made to the coal shed. M then demanded W should pay a weekly amount for the use of the coal shed. W refused.

The court found that when the lease was renewed, there was implied into the renewed lease an easement to store coal in the coal shed. All that was required was the existence of the right at the time the lease was renewed; s 62 automatically implied an easement of storage. The effect was to convert or uplift the permission/licence given by M into a full legal easement.

The conditions for the operation of s 62 are:

(1) There must be a conveyance as defined in s 205(1)(ii) LPA 1925. This requires an 'instrument', ie a written document that has the effect of creating or transferring a legal estate. For example, a mortgage or lease (including a written short-term lease not in the form of a deed). The definition excludes contracts for sale.

(2) There must be some diversity of occupation of the two parts of the land at the time of the grant. However, the requirement for some diversity does not apply:

   - to easements of light; or
   - where the rights were continuous and apparent (with the same meaning of the phrase from *Wheeldon v Burrows*) - see *P&S Platt Ltd v Crouch* [2004] 1 P & CR 242 and *Wood v Waddington* [2015] EWCA Civ 538.

   Therefore, where there is diversity of occupation, there is no requirement for the rights to be continuous and apparent.

(3) There must be an existing privilege at the date of the conveyance. Section 62 is not concerned with future rights.

(4) The right must be capable of being an easement or profit. If the right lacks the four essential characteristics of an easement in *Re Ellenborough Park*, s 62 will not cure the defect. However, the claimant does not need to demonstrate that the right is necessary for the reasonable use of the land. It is thought that s 62 applies to profits.

What to look for in a set of facts

An existing licence/permission and a subsequent conveyance. There must be diversity of occupation (but diversity is not required if the right is continuous and apparent).

Example 3.5

Harriet owned a building and annex. She leased the annex to Mohammed with an express easement allowing access using an open yard near the main buildings. During the course of the lease, Harriet gave Mohammed permission for visitors to pass through the hallway of the main building to get to the annex. A new written lease of the annex was subsequently entered into with no mention of the use of the hallway. Mohammed claimed he had an easement to use the hallway.

Would s 62 apply?

Comment

Applying the s 62 criteria to the facts:

(1) The conveyance is the second written lease.

(2) There was diversity of occupation as the building was occupied by Harriet and the annex was occupied by Mohammed.

(3) The existing privilege was the permission Harriet gave for Mohammed's visitors to pass through the hallway of the main building to access the annex.

(4) The right claimed is a well-established easement meeting the criteria in *Re Ellenborough Park*.

On this basis, the permission given by Harriet is uplifted to a full legal easement as a consequence of s 62.

These were the key facts from *Goldberg v Edwards* [1950] Ch 247 where the court followed *Wright v MacAdam* and held that an easement had been created.

3.3.6 Prescription

Where the dominant owner can show use of the right for 20 years, the court will uphold the legal right by presuming that it had a lawful origin. A legal easement is created. There are three types of prescription:

(a) at common law

(b) the doctrine of lost modern grant

(c) the Prescription Act 1832.

Whichever method is relied on it will be necessary to show that the right has been exercised by or on behalf of a fee simple owner against a fee simple owner:

1. continuously; and
2. as of right.

1. **Exercised continuously**

The user can be by a number of freehold owners in succession and may be intermittent in nature. In *Diment v N H Foot* [1974] 2 AER 785 use for six to ten occasions over a 35-year period qualified as continuous use.

2. **As of right**

The rights must be exercised without force, secrecy or permission:

Without force (nec vi)

Force would include removal of obstructions or ignoring the protests of the servient owner (whether verbal, in writing or signage).

Without secrecy (nec clam)

The user must be open and not hidden, such that a 'reasonable person in the position of the alleged servient owner, diligent in the protection of his interests, would have a reasonable opportunity of discovering the right asserted'.

In *Liverpool Corporation v Coghill* [1918] 1 Ch 307 Coghill poured borax effluent into the Corporation's sewers in the dead of night. In law this was held to be secret even though there was no deliberate attempt at concealment.

Without permission (nec precario)

Permission can be in writing or oral. Any evidence of payment to the servient landowner indicates that the user is with permission. However, mere toleration without objection will not prevent the acquisition of a prescriptive easement.

(a) **Prescription at common law**

The grant of an easement is presumed if it has been enjoyed continuously as of right since time immemorial, ie since 1189. It is presumed that a user for 20 years or more is proof of use since 1189 but this presumption can be rebutted by showing that at some time since 1189:

- the right was not exercised
- the right could not have been exercised
- the dominant and servient tenement were vested in the same owner (unity of seisin).

The presumption is, therefore, fairly simple to rebut.

(b) **Prescription under the doctrine of Lost Modern Grant**

The grant of an easement is presumed if it has been enjoyed continuously as of right for 20 years or more on the basis that there is a presumption that there was a grant of the right since 1189 but that the grant has been lost. The doctrine is a total fiction and is a last resort where it is not possible to rely on prescription at common law or under the Prescription Act 1832. This would be the situation where the dominant and servient tenements have been in common ownership since 1189 or where the user is not next before the action brought (ie there is a gap in use exceeding one year).

(c) **Prescription under the Prescription Act 1832**

If the dominant owner can show user as of right for 20 years (30 years for profits) then they will obtain a prescriptive easement even though the user clearly commenced sometime after 1189 (s 2 Prescription Act 1832).

The claimant must prove uninterrupted enjoyment for a period of at least 20 years which immediately precedes and which terminates in an action (s 4 Prescription Act 1832). The period of 20 years is counted backwards from the date of the action.

Short interruptions to the user are permitted. Any interruption in use lasting a year or more stops time running. The claimant would then have to restart the 20-year period. (If there is an interruption for more than one year, the doctrine of lost modern grant may assist.)

What to look for in a set of facts

A right that has been exercised for 20 years (30 years for profits) or more as between two distinct parcels of freehold land.

Example 3.6

In 2003, Jenny purchased 3 Lavender Lane ('the Property'). The Property was a newly built house forming part of a residential development from land acquired from a local farmer. Jenny immediately built a large conservatory on the back of the Property.

Jenny has discovered that her neighbour, Peter, who owns 5 Lavender Lane is planning to build a large two-storey extension to the rear of his house which would significantly block the light to Jenny's conservatory.

Does Jenny have a prescriptive right to light?

Comment

There is no general right to light, but the right claimed here is via a defined aperture, the conservatory. Conservatories require a great deal of natural light for their use and, therefore, Jenny should have no difficulty in demonstrating that Peter's proposed extension would infringe her right to light.

Jenny constructed the conservatory in 2003 which would mean the right has been exercised for more than 20 years. There is nothing in the facts to suggest that there has been any break in the continuity of the right or that the right has been exercised with force, secrecy or permission.

A claim for prescription via common law will fail on the basis that until 2003 the land was in one common ownership and, therefore, cannot have been exercised as an easement since time immemorial.

Jenny can base her claim either using the Prescription Act or the doctrine of lost modern grant on the basis of over 20 years use.

3.4 Extinguishment of easements

If the owner of a piece of land has the benefit of an easement over another's land, they do not have to retain it. They may, if they wish, expressly release it by deed. That will bring the easement to an end.

Similarly, as we have seen, it is not possible for a landowner to have an easement over their own land. Consequently, if they own the dominant tenement and purchase the servient tenement, the easements they have over the latter will cease.

The owner of the dominant tenement may also abandon an easement.

Example 3.7

Tom owned a house which enjoyed a right of light to certain windows in one of its walls. Tom pulled down the wall and built a replacement wall without windows. Tom then sold the house to Asha. Fourteen years later, Fred, the owner of the land next door which had the burden of the right to light, built a wall facing Asha's blank wall. Three years later, Asha created a window in the blank wall and claimed that Fred's wall was blocking her right to light.

Has Asha's right to light been abandoned?

Comment

These are the facts of *Moore v Rawson* (1824) 3 B & C 332. In this case, the court held that the right had been abandoned because by demolishing the original wall containing the windows and replacing it with a wall without windows, Tom had caused the right to light to be extinguished. If Tom had indicated an intention to put windows in the replacement wall within a reasonable time, that might have been sufficient to preserve the right. However, the fact that the replacement wall had no windows in it was a strong indication that the right was being abandoned.

Summary

- Easements and profits are capable of being legal interests.
- A deed is required to create an easement/profit but they can be created informally.
- There is no legal definition of an easement but *Re Ellenborough Park* sets out four essential characteristics for an easement:
  - there must be a dominant and servient tenement;
  - the easement must accommodate the dominant tenement;
  - the dominant and servient tenement must not be owner/occupied by the same person; and
  - the easement must be capable of forming the subject matter of the grant.
- Unlike easements, profits can exist in gross so that only the servient land need be identified.
- Easements can be implied by necessity, common intention, the rule in *Wheeldon v Burrows* and s 62 LPA to create legal easements.
- Uninterrupted user for 20 years can create legal easements by prescription (30 years for profits).

Sample questions

Question 1

The freehold owner of a detached house ('the Property') is concerned about the extension proposed by her new neighbour. The proposed extension will make parts of the Property's garden very gloomy.

Does the Property have an easement?

A Yes, the Property has an easement of light for the garden but must show an infringement.

B Yes, there is a clear easement of light which would prevent the new neighbour's development.

C No, the Property does not have an easement as no new negative easements can be created.

D No, the Property does not have an easement of light as there is no defined aperture in a garden.

E Yes, the Property has an easement to have an uninterrupted view from her garden and can stop the new neighbour's extension.

Answer

The correct option is D.

The right to light is a recognised negative easement (therefore, option C is wrong) but there is no general right to light (therefore, options A and B are wrong). A right to light must be via a defined aperture and it is hard to see how this would be a garden generally without a specific aperture benefiting from the right.

Option E is wrong as there can be no easement for an uninterrupted view.

Question 2

In 1999, a man purchased a freehold property consisting of a farm house and outbuildings including a large separate barn ('the Barn'). The Barn has its own access to the main road, but the man has always used a track ('the Track') running past the main house to access the Barn. He prefers the Track as it avoids a dangerous right-hand turn. Last year, the man sold the Barn to a woman. The transfer included an express right over the main point of access but made no mention of the Track.

Which of the following answers best describes how an easement over the Track has been created?

A This is an easement of necessity which allows the woman to access the Barn.

B This is a common intention easement and the woman can only fulfil the purpose with the easement.

C The easement is created by *Wheeldon v Burrows* as a quasi-easement in use at the time of the sale.

D The easement was expressly created in the transfer to the woman.

E The easement was created by prescription as it has been used for over 20 years.

Answer

The correct option is C.

This cannot be an easement of necessity as there is an alternative means of access and, therefore, the Barn is not landlocked. Option A is, therefore, wrong.

There is no indication of a common purpose or intention in the facts, so option B is wrong.

The transfer to the woman contained an express grant only in relation to the main point of access, not the Track. Option D is, therefore, wrong.

This cannot be an easement by prescription as, although the use started in 1999, it could not become an easement until there was a separate dominant and servient owner. This only happened when the Barn was sold last year. Option E is, therefore, wrong.

The man exercised a quasi-easement over his own land. On the transfer to the woman, this became a legal easement on the basis that the easement was clearly continuous and apparent, necessary for the reasonable enjoyment of the land (to avoid the busy junction) and in use at the time of the sale. Option C is, therefore, correct.

Question 3

A freehold owner granted a 25-year lease of their property ('the Property'). Five years after the lease was created, the freehold owner gave informal permission for the tenant to erect a sign upon the freehold owner's adjoining land advertising the tenant's business. Last month, when the lease came to an end, the tenant purchased the freehold to the Property. The transfer made no mention of the sign.

Which of the following answers best describes how an easement in relation to the sign has been created?

A The easement was created by s 62 LPA 1925 as an existing privilege upon the transfer of the freehold to the tenant.

B The easement was expressly created on the transfer of the freehold to the tenant.

C This is an easement of necessity which allows the tenant to erect a sign.

D The easement was created by prescription as it has been used for over 20 years.

E The right is not capable of existing as an easement as it does not accommodate the dominant tenement.

Answer

The correct option is A.

The easement in relation to the sign was created by implication by s 62 LPA 1925. There was an existing privilege (the freehold owner's informal permission to erect the sign), there was diversity of occupation (the freehold owner owning the servient land and the tenant occupying the Property) and there was a conveyance (the transfer of the freehold to the tenant). The effect of the conveyance is to create a legal easement in relation to the sign.

There is no mention of the easement in the transfer of the Property. Option B is, therefore, wrong.

Although the easement has been exercised for over 20 years, most of this period was whilst the Property was let. A prescriptive right can only be created as between two freehold owners. Option D is, therefore, wrong.

It is hard to consider any circumstances in which an easement relating to a sign could be an easement of necessity. Option C is, therefore, wrong.

Option E is correct in relation to the legal principle but does not answer the question asked and is, therefore, not the best answer.

4 Freehold Covenants

SQE1 syllabus

Rules for passing of the benefit and burden of freehold covenants.

Note that for SQE1, candidates are not usually required to recall specific case names or cite statutory or regulatory authorities. Cases are provided for illustrative purposes only.

Learning outcomes

By the end of this chapter you will be able to apply relevant core legal principles and rules appropriately and effectively, at the level of a competent newly qualified solicitor in practice, to realistic client-based and ethical problems and situations in the following areas:

- Understand how covenants over freehold land are created
- Distinguish between restrictive and positive covenants
- Assess the enforceability of freehold covenants at law and in equity
- Identify appropriate remedies
- Understand the options available for modification or discharge of freehold covenants.

4.1 Basics and formalities

A covenant is a promise to do or not do something. For example, a promise not to build on land.

Covenants are usually imposed when a person sells part of their land. Covenants can be imposed for a variety of reasons, but their purpose is usually to maintain or enhance the value and/or amenity of the land retained by the seller.

4.1.1 Is a covenant capable of being legal?

Covenants are not capable of being legal interests in land. They are not listed in s 1(2) LPA 1925 and are therefore equitable by nature - s 1(3) LPA 1925.

4.1.2 Formalities

As covenants are equitable by nature, the relevant formality is in writing and signed (s 53(1) LPA 1925). This means that it is possible to create a covenant by contract. However, it is usual that a covenant will be created by deed. This is because covenants tend to be created on sale of part land and are included in the transfer.

4.1.3 Terminology

Covenantor	The person who makes the promise and who has the burden of the covenant
Covenantee	The recipient of the promise and who has the benefit of the covenant
Servient land	(Or burdened land) - the land bound by the covenant owned by the covenantor
Dominant land	(Or benefited land) - the land with the benefit of the covenant owned by the covenantee
Annexation	This means that the benefit of the covenant is attached to the land of the covenantee and the benefit passes automatically to any successor in title of the covenantee
Assignment	An express transfer of the benefit of the covenant to a successor in title to the covenantee.

4.1.4 Positive vs restrictive covenants

A positive covenant requires some effort or expenditure to perform the obligation. A restrictive covenant requires no such effort or expense.

It is the substance of the covenant that will define whether or not it is positive, rather than the wording of the covenant.

Example 4.1

Read through the list of covenants and decide whether or not they are positive or restrictive:

Covenant	Positive	Restrictive
1. To keep the land as an open space.		
2. Not to divide the property into flats.		
3. Not to let the property fall into disrepair.		
4. Not to allow the grounds of the hotel to be used for public events.		
5. To contribute towards the cost of the maintenance of the shared driveway.		
6. Not to use the property other than as a single private dwelling house.		
7. To paint the exterior of the property every five years.		

Comment

The substance of the covenants in numbers 3, 5 and 7 is positive. They each require effort or expenditure to fulfil the promise. Covenant 3 is framed as a restrictive covenant, but its substance is positive.

The covenants set out in 1, 2, 4 and 6 require no effort or expense on the part of the covenantor. They are restrictive covenants.

4.1.5 Original parties

The original covenantor and the original covenantee are parties to a contract. This is therefore governed by the principles of contract law and the original covenantor is bound by privity of contract. This means that the liability of the original covenantor has the potential to last forever even after the land has been sold. The covenantor may have covenanted on behalf of themselves and their successors in title either expressly within the relevant document (usually a deed) or, if not made expressly, it can be implied by s 79 LPA 1925, provided that the covenant relates to the land.

The obligation of the original covenantor relates to both positive and restrictive covenants.

4.2 Running of the burden at common law

The burden of a covenant (whether positive or restrictive) cannot pass at common law – *Austerberry v Corporation of Oldham* (1885) 29 Ch D 750 affirmed in the House of Lords in *Rhone v Stephens* [1994] 2 AC 310.

The principle is based in contract law, where the common law rule is that only the benefit of a contract can be assigned, but never the burden. To enforce a covenant against a successor in title 'would be to enforce a personal obligation against a person who has not covenanted' per Lord Templeman in *Rhone v Stephens*.

See **4.4** below on alternative methods for enforcing a positive covenant.

Example 4.2

Roger was the freehold owner of numbers 2 and 4 Rugby Road. He sold number 4 Rugby Road ('the Property') to Sally. In the transfer, Sally covenanted with Roger to paint the exterior of the Property every three years. Sally has now sold the Property to James.

Will James be bound by the covenant?

Comment

Roger is the original covenantee and holds the benefited land, 2 Rugby Road.

Sally was the original covenantor and owner of the burdened land, the Property.

Sally is bound by privity of contract. This means that she remains bound by her promise for ever.

James is a successor in title to the original covenantor and is not bound by the covenant as the burden of a covenant cannot pass in common law.

4.3 Running of the burden in equity

The burden of a restrictive covenant may pass in equity under the doctrine in *Tulk v Moxhay* (1848) 2 Ph 774 provided that the following requirements are satisfied:

(a) the covenant must be negative (restrictive) in substance;

(b) the covenant must, at the time of the creation of the covenant, have been made to benefit dominant land retained by the covenantee;

(c) the covenant must touch and concern the dominant land;

(d) the covenant must be made with the intent to burden the servient land; and

(e) the owner of the servient land must have notice of the covenant for it to bind them (see **Chapters 7** to **9**).

(a) The covenant must be negative in substance

The rule in *Tulk v Moxhay* only applies to restrictive covenants, ie those covenants affecting the mode of using the land. **See 4.1.4** for the distinction between a positive and restrictive covenant.

(b) The covenant must, at the time of the creation of the covenant, have been made to benefit dominant land retained by the covenantee

There must be identifiable dominant land owned by the covenantee at the time the covenant is created. As most covenants are created when a part of land is sold, this means that the seller must retain land.

In *London County Council v Allen* [1914] 3 KB 642 the County Council sold land subject to a covenant not to build on it. Mrs Allen was a successor to the original covenantor and started to build on the land. The County Council could not prevent her from building as it had failed to retain any dominant land.

(c) The covenant must touch and concern the dominant land

The test created in *P & A Swift Investments v Combined English Stores Group plc* [1989] AC 632 can be used:

(i) a 'touching and concerning' covenant must benefit only the dominant owner for the time being, so that, if separated from their land, it ceases to be advantageous to them;

(ii) the covenant must affect the nature, quality, mode of user or value of the land of the dominant owner; and

(iii) the covenant must not be expressed to be personal (ie must not have been given only to one specific dominant owner).

(d) The covenant must be made with the intent to burden the servient land

The intention can either be express or implied:

Express intention

This will be set out in the document creating the covenant, for example:

> The Buyer and their successors in title covenants with the Seller to use the property only as a private dwelling house.

Implied intention

In the absence of express words, the intention can be implied using s 79(1) LPA 1925:

> A covenant relating to any land of a covenantor... Shall, unless a contrary intention is expressed, be deemed to be made by the covenantor on behalf of himself and his successors in title and the person's deriving title under him or them...

(e) The owner of the servient land must have notice of the covenant for it to bind them

How notice is given will depend upon whether the land is registered or unregistered. See **Chapters 7**, **8** and **9**.

Example 4.3

Mark owns 6 and 8 Tennyson Avenue. He sells 8 Tennyson Avenue ('the Property') to Stella. The transfer on sale to Stella contained the following clause:

'The Buyer and her successors in title covenants with the Seller to:

(a) *paint the exterior of the Property every five years; and*

(b) *not use the Property for any purpose other than a private dwelling house.'*

Stella has now sold the Property to Emma.

Is Emma bound by the covenants?

Comment

The burden of the covenants cannot run at common law (see **4.2**). However, they may run in equity if the requirements in *Tulk v Moxhay* are met. Applying these to the facts:

(a) The covenant in relation to painting the exterior of the Property requires effort/expenditure and is therefore positive. Therefore the burden does not run in equity. The covenant in relation to the use of the Property is negative/restrictive in substance and therefore runs in equity.

(b) Mark retained ownership of land that benefited from the covenant; 6 Tennyson Avenue.

(c) The restrictive covenant would be seen as a benefit to any owner of the dominant land (6 Tennyson Avenue) and arguably enhances the mode of user and value of the dominant land.

(d) The transfer contains an express intention for the burden of the covenant to run ('The Buyer and her successors in title...').

(e) Provided Emma has notice of the restrictive covenant she will be bound by it. See **Chapters 7** to **9**.

4.4 Alternative methods of enforcing a positive covenant

Positive covenants cannot run with the land, either at common law or in equity, and are therefore not enforceable against a successor in title to the covenantor. There are three devices which have evolved at common law where positive covenants can be enforced against successors in title of the servient/burdened land (either directly or indirectly):

- Create a lease
- Indemnity covenant
- The doctrine of mutual benefit and burden - *Halsall v Brizzell*

Dealing with each in turn:

4.4.1 Create a lease

Instead of selling the land freehold, the landowner can create a lease. In **Chapter 6** we will see that both restrictive and positive covenants are binding on a successor in title to a tenant. Although this ensures that positive covenants are enforceable, leases are less attractive to a buyer than the purchase of freehold land. This is because a lease must be created for a fixed duration (which will eventually come to an end) and not last forever like a freehold estate.

4.4.2 Indemnity covenant

An original covenantor remains bound by their promise as a consequence of privity of contract (see **4.1.5**). When the servient land is sold only the burdens of restrictive covenants pass to a successor in title (see **4.3**). The original covenantor therefore remains bound by positive covenants.

Upon the sale of the servient land (the land burdened by the covenant), it is normal conveyancing practice to require the buyer to enter into an indemnity covenant promising to observe positive covenants and indemnifying the seller for any loss incurred as a consequence of any breach. An indemnity covenant is then sought from each subsequent buyer of the servient land creating a chain of indemnity covenants.

In the event of the original covenantor being sued for a breach of a positive covenant (by the original covenantee or their successor in title), this enables the original covenantor to sue their successor on the indemnity and so on down the line.

It does not enable the original covenantor to sue the current owner who is in breach as there is no privity of contract between them. It is, therefore, an indirect method of enforcement.

A chain of indemnities is only as strong as its weakest link. If one person in the chain cannot be found or is insolvent then the chain is of little value and the entire burden would then fall on the last person in the chain.

Example 4.4

Bernard owned 10 and 12 Main Street. In 1990, Bernard (the original covenantee) sold 12 Main Street ('the Property') to Archie (the original covenantor), subject to a covenant to keep the Property in good repair. In 2000, Archie sold the Property to Mary. In 2014 Mary sold the Property to Gemma. Gemma has allowed the Property to fall into disrepair. In every transfer, each buyer provided an indemnity covenant in favour of each seller.

Is Gemma bound by the covenant?

Comment

The covenant is positive in substance as it involves effort and/or expenditure. The covenant does not therefore run with the burdened land (in common law or in equity), and so Bernard cannot enforce it directly against Gemma.

Archie remains bound on his promise as the original covenantor as a consequence of privity of contract. Bernard can therefore sue Archie for breach of the positive covenant.

Archie can then pursue Mary on her indemnity covenant and Mary can pursue Gemma on the indemnity covenant provided by Gemma. In this way the positive covenant can be enforced indirectly against Gemma.

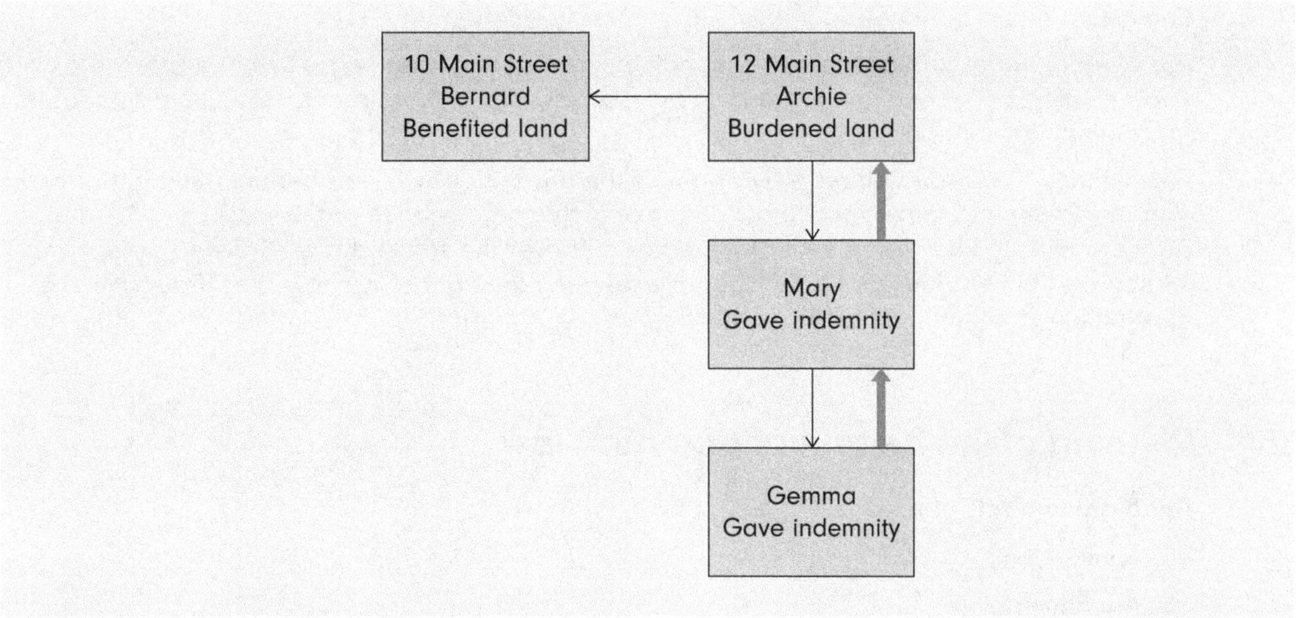

4.4.3 The doctrine of mutual benefit and burden – *Halsall v Brizell*

This doctrine dictates that a person who wishes to take advantage of a service/facility which benefits their land must also comply with any corresponding obligation. For example, to contribute towards the cost of providing and/or maintaining the service or facility – *Halsall v Brizell* [1957] Ch 169.

The doctrine has two pre-conditions as set out in *Thamesmead Town Ltd v Allotey* (2000) 79 P & CR 557:

(i) The burden must be 'relevant to the exercise of the rights which enable the benefit to be obtained'. There must be a clear correlation between the benefit and the linked burden; and

(ii) The covenantor's successors in title must have the opportunity to elect whether to take the benefit (and accept the related burden) or to renounce it (and escape the related burden).

This is not a direct method of enforcement of a positive covenant. It enables the owner of the benefited land to prevent the exercise of the rights if the costs of maintenance have not been paid.

Example 4.5

Marjorie owns a large house with extensive grounds ('the Manor House'). In 2010, she sold part of her garden to David ('the Garden Land'). Access to the Garden Land is over a track crossing the Manor House ('the Track'). The transfer to David contained the following clause:

> The Seller grants to the Buyer a right of way at all times with and without vehicles over the Track subject to the Buyer paying a contribution towards the maintenance and upkeep of the Track.

David has now sold the Garden land to Eleanor. Eleanor is refusing to pay for the upkeep of the Track.

Can Marjorie enforce the positive covenant?

Comment

The covenant to contribute towards the maintenance of the Track is positive in substance as it involves effort or expenditure to perform the obligation. It is therefore not directly enforceable (at common law or in equity).

The doctrine in *Halsall v Brizell* may apply as there is a closely linked benefit (the right of way over the Track) and burden (contribution towards the maintenance of the Track). Provided that Eleanor elects to take the benefit of the easement over the Track, she will have to accept the related burden. Marjorie can stop Eleanor exercising the right of way over the Track until the contribution to maintenance has been paid.

4.5 Running of the benefit at common law

There are two sets of rules:

- Annexation
- Assignment

4.5.1 Annexation

The original covenantee can enforce a covenant in contract. If the land benefiting from the covenant is sold, the covenantee's successor can enforce the covenant at common law if the following rules are complied with:

(a) **The covenant must touch and concern the land**

See *P & A Swift Investments v Combined English Stores Group plc* at **4.3(c)**;

(b) **There must have been an intention that the benefit should run with the estate owned by the covenantee**

This will either be by express words or implied by s 78 LPA 1925. An example of express words is:

> The Buyer and their successors in title covenant with the Seller and their successors in title...

(c) **The covenantee must have a legal estate in the benefited land**

Therefore, no benefit can pass where the original covenantee held an equitable interest.

(d) **The buyer of the benefited land must also take a legal title in the benefited land**

The decision in *Smith and Snipes Hall Farm Ltd v River Douglas Catchment Board* [1949] 2 KB 500 confirmed that the legal estate did not need to be identical and the benefit of a covenant could pass to a tenant of a legal lease.

4.5.2 Assignment

It is also possible for the benefit of a covenant to pass to a successor by express assignment. This must take place at the same time as the transfer of the land. It must be in writing and signed by the assignor (ie the original covenantee) and written notice of the assignment must be given to the person with the burden of the covenant (s 136 LPA 1925).

4.6 Running of the benefit in equity

There are three sets of rules:

- Annexation
- Assignment
- Building schemes

4.6.1 Annexation

Annexation means the permanent attachment of the covenant to the dominant land. This enables any owner of the dominant land to enforce the covenant.

There are three methods of annexation:

- Express annexation
- Implied annexation
- Statutory annexation

(a) Express annexation

The covenant should express an intention to benefit a defined piece of land (*Rogers v Hosegood* [1900] 2 Ch 388). It is not sufficient for the covenant to be made for the benefit of the covenantee and their successors in title (*Renals v Colishaw* [1879] 11Ch Div 866). Therefore, it is crucial to identify the land intended to receive the benefit of the covenant.

Provided clear words are used and the land to benefit is clearly defined the annexation should be to the whole of the dominant land, no matter how extensive.

Standard practice is to include the words 'each and every part' to ensure that the covenant is annexed to each part of the dominant land if in the future it is divided into smaller plots. Obiter comments in *Federated Homes Ltd v Mill Lodge Properties Ltd* [1980] 1 AER 371 ('*Federated Homes*') indicate that these words may no longer be needed.

Example 4.6

Amelie is the freehold owner of numbers 12 and 14 Trent View Gardens. Amelie lived at number 12 and she sold number 14 ('the Property') to Bradley. The transfer to Bradley includes the following clause:

> *For the benefit and protection of 12 Trent View Gardens and each and every part thereof the Buyer and his successors in title covenants with the Seller and her successors in title to use the Property only as a private dwelling house.*

Amelie has now sold part of number 12 to Christa ('the Garden Land')

Has the benefit of the covenant been annexed to the Garden Land?

Comment

The dominant land was originally number 12. The servient land is the Property.

Bradley is the original covenantor and Amelie the original covenantee. Christa is a successor in title to the original covenantee. Christa owns the Garden Land which formed part of number 12, the dominant land.

Words of annexation were used – 'For the benefit and protection...'

At the time of sale, the dominant land was clearly identified as being number 12.

There was a clear intention that annexation should be to each and every part of the land.

On this basis, the benefit of the covenant has been annexed to the Garden Land and any owner of the land will enjoy the benefit of the covenant.

(b) **Implied annexation**

In some situations the court has been willing to imply annexation where such annexation was obviously intended and it would be an injustice to ignore that intention. The required intention must be manifested in the transfer as construed in the light of all the surrounding circumstances (*Marten v Flight Refuelling Ltd* [1962] Ch 115).

The scope of the decision in *Federated Homes* probably renders this line of cases redundant and statutory annexation should therefore be considered in priority to implied annexation.

(c) **Statutory annexation**

The Court of Appeal held that the effect of s 78 LPA 1925 was to automatically annex a freehold covenant to each and every part of the land retained by the covenantee provided the following criteria is met:

- the covenant must have been created after the implementation of the LPA, ie post-1925; and
- the covenant must touch and concern the land. The test in *P & A Swift Investments v Combined English Stores Group plc* can be used.

The broad application of the decision in *Federated Homes* has been reduced by:

(i) the ability of the original covenanting parties to exclude the effect of s 78 LPA 1925 from the transfer creating the covenant (*Roake v Chadha* [1984] 1 WLR 40); and

(ii) the need for the land to be benefited from the covenant to be identifiable from a description, plan or other reference in the transfer, aided, if necessary, by external evidence to identify the land (*Crest Nicholson v McCallister* [2004] 1 WLR 2409).

Example 4.7

Joeeta is the freehold owner of 6 and 8 Woodbury Road. She lives in number 6. Five years ago Joeeta sold number 8 ('the Property') to Cameron. The transfer to Cameron contained the following clause:

> *For the benefit and protection of the Seller the Buyer and his successors in title covenants with the Seller and her successors in title not to keep any animals on the Property other than domestic pets.*

Elsewhere in the transfer, number 6 is identified as land being retained by Joeeta.

Last year, Cameron sold the Property to Eloise. Joeeta has now sold number 6 to Matthew.

Does Matthew have the benefit of the covenant in equity?

Comment

There is nothing in the facts to suggest that the benefit of the covenant has been assigned to Matthew.

There is no express annexation as the covenant is framed as being for the benefit of Joeeta, as the seller, and not for the benefit of number 6 (the dominant land).

Statutory annexation is likely to apply as:

- the covenant was created post-1925 so after the implementation of the LPA 1925;
- the covenant touches and concerns the land applying the test from *P & A Swift Investments v Combined English Stores Group plc* (the covenant would cease to be a benefit once the land was sold, any owner of the land would benefit from the covenant and it is not expressed to be personal); and
- the land which benefits from the covenant is identified in the transfer.

4.6.2 Assignment

As with the passing of the benefit of a covenant at common law, it is possible for the benefit of a covenant to pass to a successor in equity by express assignment and the same conditions apply (see **4.5.2**).

4.6.3 Building schemes

Building schemes are relatively rare and modern developments tend to exclude them. The characteristics of a building scheme are:

- it applies to a defined area where title is derived from a common owner;
- the estate was laid out in lots subject to restrictions intended to be imposed on all the lots;
- the common owner intended the restrictions to apply to all the lots to be sold; and
- the original buyers bought their lots on the basis that the restrictions would benefit all of the lots in the scheme.

The effect is to impose reciprocal obligations between the buyers of the different plots of the scheme, including positive covenants.

4.7 Matching the benefit and burden

A covenant is enforceable (positive or restrictive) as between the original contracting parties. When both the dominant and servient land has changed hands, how the benefit and burden have passed needs to match for the dominant land owner to take action. The approach depends on whether the covenant is positive or restrictive:

Restrictive covenant

When the original covenantor sells the servient land the burden of a restrictive covenant cannot pass at common law (see **4.2**). The burden may pass in equity if the criteria in *Tulk v Moxhay* is met (see **4.3**).

When the original covenantee sells the dominant land the successor in title needs to demonstrate that they have the benefit of the covenant in equity. This will enable them to pursue a claim (in equity) against the successor in title to the original covenantor.

Example 4.8

Maurice is the freehold owner of 14 and 16 Barnet Crescent. Maurice lives at number 14. Ten years ago, Maurice sold number 16 ('the Property') to Louise. The transfer to Louise contained the following covenant:

> *For the benefit and protection of 14 Barnet Crescent the Buyer and her successors in title covenant with the Seller and his successors in title to use the Property only as a private dwelling house.*

Eight years ago, Louise sold the Property to Desmond. Maurice sold number 14 to Amanda. Last year, Desmond sold the Property to Ola.

Ola is running her physiotherapy business from the Property.

Can Amanda take action in respect of the breach of covenant?

Comment

The original covenantor is Louise and the original covenantee is Maurice. The dominant land is number 14 and the servient land is the Property.

Has the burden of the covenant passed?

The burden of the covenant cannot pass at common law. It may pass in equity if the criteria in *Tulk v Moxhay* is met. Applying this to the facts:

(a) the covenant is restrictive in substance as it requires no effort or expenditure in order to perform it;

(b) Maurice retained ownership of land that benefited from the covenant, ie number 14;

(c) the restrictive covenant would be seen as a benefit to any owner of the dominant land (number 14) and arguably enhances the mode of user and value of the dominant land;

(d) the transfer contains an express intention for the burden of the covenant to run ('The Buyer and her successors in title...'); and

(e) provided Ola (the current owner of the servient land) has notice of the restrictive covenant she will be bound by it. See **Chapters 7** to **9**.

Has the benefit of the covenant passed?

As the covenant is restrictive, the burden of the covenant only passes in equity. Therefore, Amanda must demonstrate that she has the benefit of the covenant in equity.

There is nothing to suggest on the facts that the benefit of the covenant has been expressly assigned.

There are words of annexation in the covenant ('For the benefit and protection...') which clearly identifies the benefited land (number 14).

Amanda therefore has the benefit of the covenant in equity and can pursue Ola for breach of covenant if Ola is bound by the covenant in equity as a consequence of *Tulk v Moxhay*.

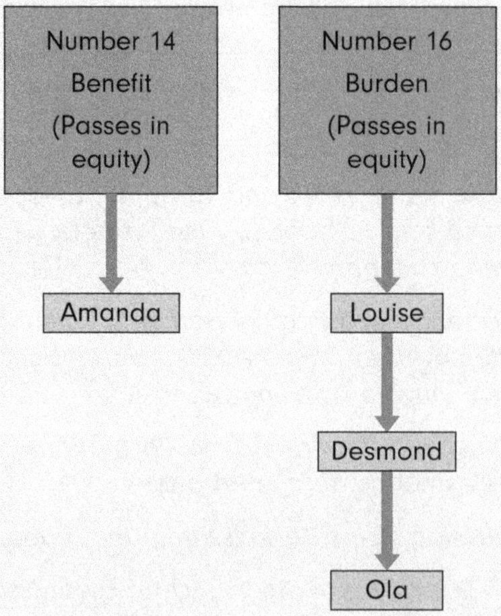

Positive covenant

When the original covenantor sells the servient land the burden of a positive covenant cannot pass to a successor in title either at common law or in equity. The original covenantor remains bound by privity of contract in relation to positive covenants.

A successor in title to the dominant land can pursue the original covenantor for breach of a positive covenant provided that the successor in title can show that the benefit of the positive covenant has passed to them at common law (see **4.5**).

The original covenantor may then be able to pursue their own successor in title via an indemnity covenant (see **4.4.2**).

Example 4.9

Tom is the freehold owner of 22 and 24 May Road. Tom sells number 24 ('the Property') to Caitlin. The transfer to Caitlin contains the following clause:

> *The Buyer and her successors in title covenant with the Seller and his successors in title not to allow the Property to fall into disrepair.*

Caitlin sells the Property to Siobhan. Tom sells number 22 to Archie. Siobhan has allowed the Property to fall into disrepair.

Can Archie pursue Caitlin for the breach of covenant?

Comment

Although framed as a restrictive covenant, the covenant is positive in substance. It requires effort or expenditure in order to perform it.

The burden of a positive covenant cannot pass to a successor in title by either common law or equity. Caitlin remains bound on her promise as a consequence of privity of contract as the original covenantor.

Archie can pursue Caitlin on her promise provided that he can show that he has the benefit of the covenant at common law (see **4.5**).

4.8 Remedies for breach of covenant

The remedies available depend on the nature of the covenant and who has breached it.

4.8.1 Positive covenant

Damages are the usual common law remedy for a breach of a positive covenant. They can be sought against the original covenantor by the original covenantee or a successor in title to the original covenantee (provided that they have the benefit of the covenant at common law - see **4.5**).

Damages provide a purely monetary solution and may include a sum for future loss. Once the original covenantee has disposed of the land benefiting from the covenant, they would be unable to demonstrate that they have suffered a loss and would therefore be unable to claim damages.

Specific performance may be available for the breach of a positive covenant by the original covenantor (but not a successor in title to the original covenantor). However, the original covenantor will have no control over the land, so can pay, but not necessarily perform the obligation.

4.8.2 Restrictive covenant

A restrictive covenant only runs with the land in equity meaning that the principal remedy is an injunction. There is no automatic right to an injunction.

The purpose of an injunction is to restrain the breach of a restrictive covenant. An injunction can be applied for in anticipation of a breach or in response to an existing breach.

An injunction is an equitable remedy and therefore within the discretion of the court. A court will award damages for breach of a restrictive covenant instead of an injunction where:

- the injury to the claimant's rights are small
- and capable of being estimated in money
- and can be adequately compensated by money; and
- it would be oppressive to the respondent to grant an injunction (*Shelfer v City of London Electric Lighting Co* (1895) 1 Ch 287).

It would be oppressive where, for example, homes have been built, sold and occupied in breach of a restrictive covenant. In that situation, a court is more likely to use its discretion to award damages. However, if the breach is in flagrant disregard of the terms of the covenant and/or the objections by the owner of the dominant land, the court may be less sympathetic to an argument of oppression.

The Supreme Court in *Coventry v Lawrence* [2014] UKSC 13 has indicated that the court should have regard to broader considerations than the test in *Shelfer* when exercising its discretion. However, where an injunction would be oppressive, an award of damages was more likely.

An injunction will not be awarded where the claimant has acted inequitably or has delayed action (*Gafford v Graham* [1999] 41 EG 159). In addition, he who seeks equity must do so with clean hands.

It is possible for the person with the benefit of a restrictive covenant to pursue a claim against the original covenantee based in privity of contract. However, that claim would be for damages only and therefore unlikely to provide an adequate remedy.

4.9 Modification and discharge of restrictive covenants

The methods of removing or limiting the effect of a freehold covenant are:

- express release
- common ownership
- s 84 LPA 1925
- insurance

Express release

The covenantee(s) may agree to release or modify a covenant (restrictive or positive). A deed is required, entered into by the owners of the servient and dominant land. Payment (or some other value) is usually negotiated for such a release.

Common ownership

Where the servient and dominant land come into common ownership, the covenant (restrictive or positive) will be extinguished. This is also called unity of seisin.

Section 84 LPA 1925

This applies only to restrictive covenants. An application can be made to the Lands Chamber of the Upper Tribunal ('the Lands Chamber') to discharge or modify the covenant in whole or in part. The burden is on the applicant to satisfy one of the grounds in s 84(1) LPA 1925. The Lands Chamber may make an order if it is satisfied that one of the conditions in s 84(1) LPA 1925 is fulfilled:

(a) the restrictive covenant was found to be obsolete; or

(aa) the restrictive covenant impedes some reasonable use of the land and either:

(i) it does not secure any practical benefit or value to the persons it should benefit; or

(ii) it is contrary to the public interest

and in either case, money will be adequate compensation; or

(b) that those entitled to the benefit have expressly or impliedly agreed to the discharge; or

(d) that the discharge will not injure the persons entitled to the benefit.

Where the identity of the dominant owners is not certain, a preliminary application can be made to the court under s 84(2) LPA 1925 to establish the identity of the dominant owner(s).

Insurance

This relates to restrictive covenants only. An insurance policy is purchased for a one-off premium. In the event of the dominant owner(s) seeking to enforce the breach of a restrictive covenant, the insurer accepts the financial risks of such action.

Summary

- Covenants are not capable of being legal.
- Covenants can be created by being in writing and signed.
- A covenant that requires effort or expense for its performance is positive in substance.
- The original covenantor is bound by privity of contract.
- The burden of a positive covenant cannot pass to a successor in title to the original covenantor.
- The burden of a restrictive covenant can pass in equity if the criteria in *Tulk v Moxhay* is met.
- Positive covenants may be indirectly enforced using the doctrine of mutual benefit and burden or a chain of indemnity covenants.
- The benefit of a covenant can pass at common law.
- The benefit of a covenant can pass in equity (relevant for restrictive covenants).
- If the burden has passed in equity it must be matched by the benefit passing in equity (restrictive covenant).
- If a successor to the original covenantee wishes to purse the original covenantor for breach of a covenant, they must show they have the benefit at common law.
- Remedies for the breach of a positive covenant are damages and possible specific performance.
- Remedies for the breach of a restrictive covenant are injunction or damages in lieu of an injunction.
- Covenants can be released or modified by agreement, common ownership or (in the case of restrictive covenant) by an application to the Lands Chamber.

Sample questions

Question 1

The freehold owner of a farm (the seller) sells a field containing a barn forming part of the farm ('the Property') to a buyer. The transfer to the buyer contains the following:

> The Buyer covenants with the Seller to repair and maintain the barn forming part of the Property.

Which of the following statements best describes the right created by the seller and the buyer?

A The positive covenant is a legal interest as it has been created by deed.

B The restrictive covenant is an equitable interest although it has been created by deed.

C The positive covenant is an equitable interest although it has been created by deed.

D The restrictive covenant is a legal interest as it has been created by deed.

E This creates an easement in favour of the buyer to access the barn forming part of the Property.

Answer

The correct option is C.

A covenant is not capable of being legal (s 1(3) LPA 1925). Creation by deed does not alter this. Options A and D are, therefore, wrong.

The covenant in question is positive as it will require effort or expenditure to perform it. Option B is, therefore, wrong.

Option E is wrong as a covenant has clearly been created, not an easement.

Question 2

A barrister is the freehold owner of two houses. He lives in one house (the 'Retained Land'). He sells the other house ('the Property') to an architect. The transfer contains the following clause:

> For the benefit and protection of the Retained Land the Buyer and his successors in title covenant with the Seller and his successors in title to only use the Property as a private dwelling house.

The architect sells the Property to a doctor. The barrister sells the Retained Land to a vet. The doctor sells the Property to a friend.

Which of the following answer best describes the parties to the various transactions?

A The barrister is the original covenantee and the vet owns the land burdened by the covenant.

B The barrister is the original covenantor and the friend owns the land burdened by the covenant.

C The architect is the original covenantee and the friend owns the land which benefits from the covenant.

D The architect is the original covenantor and the vet owns the land which benefits from the covenant.

E The architect is the original covenantor and the barrister owns the land which benefits from the covenant.

Answer

The correct option is D.

The architect is the original covenantor. Option C is, therefore, wrong.

The friend now owns the land burdened by the covenant - the Property.

The original covenantee was the barrister. Option B is, therefore, wrong.

The vet now owns the land that benefits from the covenant. Option A is, therefore, wrong.

Option E is wrong as, although the architect is the original covenantor, the barrister no longer owns the land benefitting from the covenant.

Question 3

A market research analyst is the freehold owner of two houses. The analyst sells one house ('the Property') to an occupational therapist. The transfer to the occupational therapist contained the following clause:

> The Buyer and her successors in title covenant with the Seller and his successors in title to use the Property only as a private dwelling house.

Elsewhere in the transfer, the other house is identified as the seller's 'Retained Land'. The occupational therapist has sold the Property to a recruitment consultant. The market research analyst has sold his house to a teacher. The recruitment consultant has started running a business from the Property in breach of the covenant.

Which of the following answers best describes the basis upon which the teacher has the benefit of the covenant?

A There has been an express assignment of the benefit of the covenant to the teacher.

B There is statutory annexation as the land to be benefited is identified in the transfer.

C The benefit passes to the teacher at common law as the criteria are met.

D There is express annexation as words of annexation have been used.

E There is a mutual benefit and burden enabling the teacher to enforce the covenant.

Answer

The correct option is B.

There is nothing in the facts to suggest that there has been express assignment. Option A is wrong.

There is no express annexation as words of annexation have not been used and the land to benefit from the covenant is not identified in the clause creating the covenant. Option D is wrong.

Option C is accurate as the benefit will have passed to the teacher at common law. However, the covenant is restrictive and, therefore, the burden will only pass in equity. In order for the teacher to pursue a claim, the teacher must show that benefit of the covenant has passed to her in equity. Option C is, therefore, not the best answer.

There is nothing on the facts to suggest a mutual benefit and burden. This only applies to positive covenants and here the covenant is restrictive. Option E is, therefore, wrong.

For these reasons, the only way in which the benefit of the covenant can pass to the teacher is by way of statutory annexation.

5 Mortgages

SQE1 syllabus

Mortgages including:

- Enforceability of terms
- Lenders' powers and duties
- Protection of mortgagors

Priority of mortgages and protection of third parties with an interest in the land are dealt with in **Chapters 8 and 9**.

Note that for SQE1, candidates are not usually required to recall specific case names or cite statutory or regulatory authorities. Cases are provided for illustrative purposes only.

Learning outcomes

By the end of this chapter you will be able to apply relevant core legal principles and rules appropriately and effectively, at the level of a competent newly qualified solicitor in practice, to realistic client-based and ethical problems and situations in the following areas:

- Understand what a mortgage is
- Explain how a legal mortgage is created
- Assess the remedies available to a lender
- Identify the duties of a lender in enforcing its remedies
- Understand the protection afforded to borrowers.

5.1 What is a mortgage?

People commonly use the term 'mortgage' to describe the money advanced by a lender to a borrower to help them purchase a property. In reality, the lender provides money by way of a loan and, in return, the borrower provides security by creating a mortgage over the property in favour of the lender.

When a mortgage is created the borrower continues to hold the legal estate (freehold or leasehold) subject to the mortgage. A mortgage is therefore a third party right over land. See **Chapters 7** to **9**.

The creation of a mortgage enables the lender to enforce its security against the borrower. There are a number of remedies available to a lender (see **5.5**) with a number of protections for the borrower.

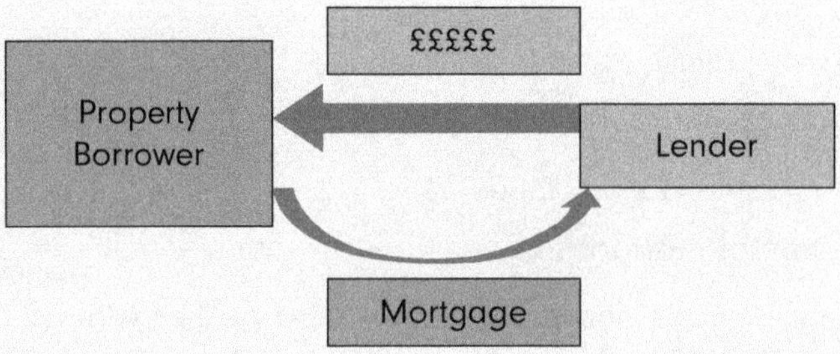

5.2 Is a mortgage capable of being legal?

Mortgages are capable of being legal interests in land. They are listed in s 1(2)(c) LPA 1925 and described as a charge by way of legal mortgage. The terms mortgage and charge are used interchangeably.

5.3 Formalities

A deed is required to create a legal mortgage in relation to a legal estate (freehold or leasehold) – s 52(1) LPA 1925. The deed must meet the requirements set out in s 1 LPMPA 1989.

As a mortgage is capable of being a legal interest, where the document lacks the requirements of a deed, equity may intervene and recognise an equitable mortgage under the principle of *Walsh v Lonsdale*.

A mortgage can be created over an equitable interest. This would need to comply with s 53(1) LPA 1925 – in writing and signed. For example, when a co-owner of land creates a mortgage in relation to their equitable interest under a trust.

5.4 Terminology

Mortgage	(Or charge) interest over land granted as security for a loan. If the borrower fails to repay the loan, the lender can enforce its security
Mortgagor	(Or borrower) the owner of the estate in land borrowing a sum of money and giving the lender a mortgage as security for the loan
Mortgagee	(Or lender) has the benefit of the mortgage enabling them to enforce their security

5.5 Lenders' powers and duties and protection of mortgagors

The focus in this chapter is on the remedies available to a lender in relation to a legal mortgage. The remedies available in relation to an equitable mortgage are beyond the scope of this manual.

It is entirely for the lender to decide which remedy to pursue; although, in so doing, the lender must avoid a course of action that would substantially increase the burden to the borrower. The remedies available are:

- possession
- the power of sale
- debt action
- appointing a receiver
- foreclosure

Only exercise of the power of sale and foreclosure will bring the mortgage to an end. The right to possession is usually used as a precursor to the exercise of another remedy (usually either exercising the power of sale or appointing a receiver).

5.5.1 Possession

The lender has the right to take possession 'before the ink is dry on the mortgage' – *Four Maids Ltd v Dudley Marshall (Properties) Ltd* [1957] Ch 317.

The borrower does not need to be in default for the lender to exercise its right of possession. Possession means either:

- taking physical possession (ousting the borrowers); or
- where the property is let, directing that the tenants pay their rent to the lender (rather than the borrower).

In practice, lenders will only exercise this right if the borrower is in default. Possession is rarely used in isolation. It is usually used with other remedies, for example as a pre-cursor to exercising the power of sale or the appointment of a receiver.

The lender cannot use or threaten violence towards anyone known to be present on the property in order to obtain possession (s 6 Criminal Law Act 1977). If a lender can retake possession without breach of s 6 of the Criminal Law Act, a court order for possession is not required (*Ropaigealach v Barclays Bank Plc* [2000] 1 QB 263). This will usually only be when the property is empty (or when the property is let and the lender directs the tenants to pay rent to the lender).

Possession without a court order was challenged on ECHR Art 8 grounds in *Horsham Properties Group Ltd v Clark* [2008] EWHC 2327 (Ch). The court found that possession following a default was justified in the public interest and reflected the nature of the necessary security which a mortgagee needed to offer substantial lending on property at affordable rates of interest.

Possession proceedings

Where the property is residential, the lender must comply with the pre-action protocol. This promotes an open dialogue between lender and borrower to attempt to resolve any arrears prior to seeking possession. This includes considering selling the property or re-scheduling the debt with the aim of avoiding possession proceedings. The pre-action protocol is weighted in favour of enabling the borrower to continue to make payments and live in the property.

Section 36 of the Administration of Justice Act (AJA) 1970 (as amended by s 8 AJA 1973) allows the borrower to ask the court to exercise its discretion to:

- adjourn proceedings; or
- on making an order for possession, suspend execution or postpone the date for possession.

Section 36 AJA 1970 applies when:

(a) the lender has started possession proceedings;

(b) the property includes a dwelling-house; and

(c) the borrower is likely within a reasonable period to pay any sums due under the mortgage (ie arrears).

The court will not exercise its discretion unless the borrower can provide a detailed financial plan demonstrating that they can pay both the mortgage instalments as they fall due and any arrears.

A reasonable period has been defined to include the full remaining period of the mortgage (*Cheltenham and Gloucester Building Society v Norgan* [1996] 1 WLR 343).

Example 5.1

Wendy purchased and moved into 14 Hope Crescent ('the Property') five years ago with the aid of a 25-year loan from East Central Bank Plc ('the Bank'). She duly granted the Bank a mortgage over the Property (by deed). Wendy lost her job six months ago and has not paid the monthly mortgage payments for four months. Wendy has just started a new, better paid, job and believes that she will be able to catch up with the arrears. The Bank have now started proceedings for possession.

What protection does Wendy have?

Comment

The mortgage was created by deed and is therefore a legal mortgage. The Bank have the right to take possession at any time but must not use violence or threats of violence to do so.

The Bank must obtain a court order for possession as the Property is a dwelling house occupied by Wendy. As part of those proceedings, Wendy can ask the court to exercise its discretion in s 36 AJA 1970 to adjourn the proceedings or stay or suspend the effect of any order. The reasonable period referred to in s 36 AJA 1970 will be the remaining 20 years of the mortgage. This means that Wendy can spread the payment of the arrears over that 20-year period, but must show that she can pay both the usual monthly mortgage payments and the arears.

Strict duty to account

Where the property subject to the mortgage is producing income, the lender can use the income to pay the debt owed. However, the lender must:

(a) account to the borrower for any sum beyond that which is due to them; and

(b) manage the property with due diligence, accounting to the borrower for any income that should have been received had the property been managed correctly.

This strict duty to account is why lenders prefer to appoint a receiver in relation to an income-producing property (see **5.5.4**).

5.5.2 The power of sale

Before exercising the power of sale, the lender may need to obtain possession of the property.

The power of sale must:

- exist;
- have arisen; and
- become exercisable.

The power of sale exists

The power of sale is either expressly stated within the mortgage deed or implied into every legal mortgage (provided that the power has not been excluded) (s 101 LPA 1925).

The power of sale must have arisen

For the power of sale to have arisen, the mortgage money must be due. This means that the legal date for redemption has passed (usually one month into the mortgage term) or any instalment of the mortgage money has become due under an instalment mortgage. Instalment mortgages are the norm for residential mortgages. The legal date for redemption, however, will usually be expressed in the mortgage deed.

The power of sale must be exercisable

This will either be set out expressly in the mortgage deed or the lender will rely on one of the elements in s 103 LPA 1925 as follows:

(i) the lender has given the borrower notice to repay the loan amount and the borrower has not paid the sum for three months after such notice; or

(ii) interest is in arrears for two months after becoming due; or

(iii) the borrower has breached a term of the mortgage (other than the covenant to pay the mortgage money or the interest thereon).

The notice referred to in (i) above is a notice given to the borrower by the lender asking for the entire debt to be repaid. Borrowers pay their mortgage by monthly instalments. Each instalment includes a monthly interest payment. The power of sale becomes exercisable if the borrower fails to pay two months of mortgage payments. The mortgage will include obligations on the part of the borrower to, for example, insure the property and keep it in good repair. Breach of such an obligation would make the power of sale exercisable.

Example 5.2

Murray is the freehold owner of 16 Castle Mews ('the Property'). The property is subject to a mortgage in favour of Notts Bank Plc ('the Bank') which was made by deed five years ago. Murray is struggling financially and has not paid his monthly mortgage payments for four months.

Can the Bank exercise the power of sale?

Comment

The mortgage is capable of being legal (s 1(2)(c) LPA 1925) and has been made by deed (s 52(1) LPA 1925) in accordance with s 1 LPMPA 1989. The power of sale is implied into every mortgage created by deed.

As the mortgage was created five years ago, it is likely that the legal date for redemption has passed, and so, the power of sale has arisen. Murray has four months' arrears of interest payments meaning that the power of sale is exercisable under s 103 LPA 1925.

Lender's duties on sale

Before selling, the lender must ensure that the power of sale has arisen and become exercisable. Conversely, the buyer only needs to check that the power of sale exists and has arisen. The buyer does not need to check that the power has become exercisable (s 104 LPA 1925).

The purpose of the sale is to recover the funds owed to the lender which are tied up in the property. The lender has the choice of when and how to sell. This could be via private treaty (ie negotiating with buyers individually using an agent) or auction. However, lenders owe duties (in equity) to borrowers (and all others interested in the equity of redemption) when exercising their power of sale. A lender must:

(a) act in good faith and not cheat borrowers (eg the property must be properly advertised and the lender cannot sell hastily at a knock down price); and

(b) take reasonable care to obtain the true market value of the property at the date of sale. Lenders are not under any obligation to delay the sale in order to maximise the price of the property.

The 'equity of redemption' is the right (in equity) for the borrower to recover the assets subject to the mortgage upon repayment of the debt. If the property is worth more than the sum owed, the balance, payable to the borrower, represents the equity of redemption.

Market values of property can vary and be difficult to estimate so 'provided the lender has exposed the property to the market properly and fairly' it will have discharged its duty.

If the lender fails to obtain the true value, it must account to the borrower (and all others with an interest in the equity of redemption) for the difference. The onus of proof is on the borrower to show that there has been a breach of the duty of care.

Example 5.3

Cuckmere Brick Co Ltd was the freehold owner of a large vacant site subject to a mortgage in favour of Mutual Finance Co Ltd. Cuckmere had planning permission to develop the site either for houses or flats. Cuckmere fell into financial difficulties and the lender exercised its power of sale, selling the property at auction. The adverts for the auction only mentioned the planning permission for houses. This would make the property less attractive to prospective buyers as the profits on a development of houses are lower than that for flats.

Comment

These are the key facts from *Cuckmere Brick Co Ltd v Mutual Finance Co Ltd* [1971] Ch 949 where the court found that the lender had failed to obtain the true market value. The lender had to account to Cuckmere for the difference in value between the price that could have been achieved (if the property had been properly advertised) less the price obtained.

Effect of sale

When a lender exercises its power of sale the buyer of the property takes the whole estate of the borrower:

(a) free of any estates or interests (including other mortgages) which the selling lender took priority over; but

(b) subject to any estates and interests which took priority over the selling lender.

The effect of the sale of mortgaged property by a lender is dealt with under s 104 LPA 1925 and will be considered in more detail in **Chapter 8**.

Proceeds of sale

The selling lender is a trustee of the proceeds of sale and must distribute them in accordance with s 105 LPA 1925 to pay:

(a) the costs of redeeming any prior mortgages (ie mortgages with priority over the selling lender's mortgage);

(b) the lender's expenses of sale;

(c) the lender's own mortgage; and

(d) the balance (if any) to the person(s) entitled to the equity of redemption (ie a subsequent lender and/or the borrower).

Example 5.4

Beth purchased 54 St Mary's Close ('the Property') six years ago for £275,000 with the assistance of a loan from Melton Bank Plc ('the Bank'). Beth granted the Bank a mortgage over the Property (made by deed). Beth fell into financial difficulties and was in six months arrears with her mortgage payments when the Bank exercised its power of sale and sold the Property at auction for £270,000. The sale was during a downturn in the market. Beth had obtained planning permission to convert the Property into four flats but this was not mentioned in the advertising for the auction. Beth believes the Property could have sold for a much higher figure had the planning permission been mentioned and the Bank had waited until the market improved.

Has the Bank breached its duties in relation to the exercise of its power of sale?

Comment

- The mortgage is capable of being legal and has been made by deed.
- The power of sale is implied into every mortgage made by deed (s 101 LPA).
- The legal date of redemption will have passed as the mortgage was made six years ago.
- The power of sale was exercisable as there were more than two months of unpaid interest payments (s 103 LPA).
- The Bank can choose when to sell the Property and is not obliged to wait for an increase in property values.
- The Bank must take reasonable care to obtain the true market value of the property at the date of sale. This may not be the case if the planning permission was not advertised prior to the auction.
- The onus is on Beth to show that the Property could have reached a higher price than the price achieved by the Bank. If so, the Bank would have to account to Beth for the difference between what could have been achieved and the sale price of £270,000.

5.5.3 Debt action

This is to recover the debt by an action for repayment on the borrower's covenant to pay. The legal date for redemption must have passed before action can be taken. See **5.5.2**.

The Limitation Act 1980 limits the lender's ability to recover the debt to:

- six years for the recovery of interest; and
- twelve years for the recovery of capital.

Where a lender has exercised the power of sale and the proceeds of sale are insufficient to pay the debt (negative equity), the lender can pursue the borrower for the shortfall as a debt action.

5.5.4 Appointment of a receiver

A lender will usually only appoint a receiver if the property subject to the mortgage is producing income, for example let to tenants. The power arises in the same way as the power of sale (see **5.5.2**) and therefore the power must exist, have arisen and be exercisable – s 109(1) LPA 1925. The receiver must be appointed in writing and it is for the lender to decide who to appoint.

The receiver has the power to demand and receive income from the property. Such income must be applied as per s 109(8) LPA 1925 to pay:

- outgoings on the property;
- interest on any prior mortgages;
- insurance premiums, repair costs and their own costs;
- interest on the current mortgage;
- capital on the current mortgage; and
- the balance to the borrower.

The LPA 1925 does not grant the receiver any power to sell the property. The terms of the mortgage will usually extend the powers of the receiver to include a power to sell the property (and may stipulate that the receiver is appointed by deed).

Receiver as agent of the borrower

A receiver is deemed to be the agent of the borrower (s 109(2) LPA 1925) and the borrower is solely responsible for the acts of the receiver. The practical effect is that the borrower has no recourse to the lender for the acts or omissions of the receiver.

This makes appointing a receiver more attractive to a lender than taking possession. The lender escapes the strict duty to account in taking possession and liability is passed to the receiver.

Duties of a receiver

A receiver owes their duties to the appointing lender, but has duties in relation to both the lender and borrower as follows:

(a) to ensure that their personal interests do not conflict with their role as a receiver. Therefore, a receiver cannot purchase the mortgaged property in a personal capacity;

(b) to act in good faith in the course of their appointment;

(c) to act with reasonable competence. What this means depends on the nature of the particular property. For example, where a receiver takes over the running of a pig farm, they should negotiate the usual trade discounts on pig feed;

(d) to take reasonable care to obtain the true market value of the property at the date of sale (if the receiver has the power of sale); and

(e) the receiver may (but is not obliged to) take steps to increase the value of the property (ie obtaining planning permission or letting the property).

These duties extend to any other person with an interest in the equity of redemption. However, if the interests of the lender and borrower conflict, the receiver is permitted to put the interests of the lender first.

Example 5.5

Emily purchased a three-storey office block ('the Property') five years ago with the aid of a mortgage (by deed) with Burnley Bank Plc ('the Bank'). The deed extended the powers of a receiver to include the power of sale. Emily let two floors of the Property to a tenant but one floor remained vacant. Emily has not paid any mortgage payments for three months and the Bank appointed a receiver. The receiver sold the Property at auction without first letting the vacant floor.

Emily wants to take action against the Bank as she believes a better price could have been obtained.

Comment

The power to appoint a receiver arises in the same way as the power of sale. Here the power of sale exists (the mortgage was by deed), the legal redemption date has passed (likely as the mortgage was created five years ago) and the power has become exercisable (Emily is in three months' arrears).

The receiver is deemed to be Emily's agent and, therefore, Emily can only pursue the receiver, not the Bank.

The receiver is under the same duties as a lender in exercising the power of sale. Hence, the receiver can choose the timing and is under no obligation to increase the value of the Property prior to the sale.

5.5.5 Foreclosure

Foreclosure is available by an application to the High Court once the legal date for redemption has passed. The process is in two stages:

(i) **Foreclosure Nisi** directing the preparation of accounts of what is owed followed by a period of (usually) six months in which to pay; and

(ii) **Foreclosure Absolute** which has the effect of vesting title to the property in the lender and extinguishing the equity of redemption held by the borrower.

If the property is worth more than the sum owed, the lender is entitled to keep the surplus. Conversely, if the property is worth less than the sum owed the borrower is released from liability. Hence, a lender would not use this remedy where there was negative equity.

Protection for the borrower

The borrower is protected from the draconian effect of foreclosure by:

(a) the discretion of the court to re-open foreclosure proceedings, in exceptional circumstances, even after the foreclosure absolute order; or

(b) where the property is a dwelling house, the borrower may seek to adjourn the foreclosure proceedings by means of an application under the AJA 1970 (see **5.5.1**); or

(c) an application to court for a judicial sale under s 91(2) LPA 1925. This will preserve the equity of redemption in favour of the borrower. Such an application can be made by any person with an interest in the equity of redemption. For example, another mortgagee.

The term 'foreclosure' is often used in popular dramas but rarely means the remedy of foreclosure. What is usually referred to here is the lender exercising its power of sale.

Summary

- A mortgage is granted by the borrower in favour of the lender as security for a loan.
- A mortgage is capable of being a legal interest.
- A mortgage must be created by deed in order to be legal.
- A lender has an automatic right to possession but if the property is occupied as a dwelling a court order will be required and the borrower can seek the protection of the AJA 1970.
- The power of sale is exercisable only when certain criteria have been met and the lender is bound by certain duties when exercising it. Exercising the power of sale will end the mortgage.
- A lender can pursue the borrower via a debt action.
- The lender can appoint a receiver in the same circumstances as exercising the power of sale and subject to the same duties but the receiver is deemed to be the agent of the borrower.
- A lender can foreclose a mortgage which brings the mortgage to an end and vests the title in the lender. There are protections for the borrower to avoid foreclosure.

Sample questions

Question 1

A borrower purchased a house ('the Property') four years ago with the assistance of a mortgage (by deed) with a bank ('the Bank'). The borrower has been made redundant and has not paid the last mortgage payment. The Bank want to sell the Property immediately.

Which of the following statements most accurately describes the position for the Bank?

A The buyer need only check that that the power of sale exists and has arisen.

B The Bank can exercise the power of sale as it exists, has arisen and is exercisable.

C The Bank cannot exercise the power of sale as the power of sale does not exist.

D The Bank cannot exercise the power of sale as the power is not yet exercisable.

E The buyer will take the Property subject to the mortgage in favour of the Bank.

Answer

The correct option is D.

The power of sale exists (the mortgage was made by deed) and has arisen (the mortgage was made four years ago so the legal date for redemption will have passed). Therefore, option C is wrong.

The power of sale is not exercisable as the borrower has only failed to pay one monthly payment, not two. Option B is, therefore, wrong.

Option A correctly states the legal position but does not answer the question and is, therefore, wrong.

Option E is wrong. A buyer would take free of the Bank's mortgage upon the Bank exercising the power of sale.

Although the power of sale exists and has arisen, the power is not yet exercisable as there is not yet two months' arrears. Option D is, therefore, correct.

Question 2

A solicitor acts for the freehold owner of a vacant office block ('the Property') subject to a mortgage (by deed) in favour of a bank ('the Bank'). The owner purchased the Property five years ago on a 25-year mortgage. The owner has not paid the mortgage payments for the last two months after their tenant's lease came to an end and the tenant vacated the Property. The Bank have told the owner that they plan to exercise their power of sale in relation to the Property. The owner wishes to oppose this as there is a downturn in the market and it is a dreadful time to sell.

Can the owner oppose the Bank in exercising its power of sale?

A Yes, because the Bank must obtain a court order for possession prior to selling the Property.

B No, because the power of sale is exercisable and the Property is not a dwelling house.

C Yes, because the owner can apply to the court to adjourn the possession proceedings.

D No, because the Bank can choose the timing of the sale but must obtain a possession order for possession.

E Yes, because the Bank's power of sale is not exercisable until the owner is in arrears for three months.

Answer

The correct option is B.

The power of sale exists (the mortgage was created by deed), has arisen (the mortgage was created five years ago and the date for redemption should have passed) and is exercisable as the owner is in two months' arrears of interest payments. Option E is, therefore, wrong as only two months of arrears are needed.

The Bank do not need to obtain a possession order as this is not a dwelling house and the Property is vacant. Therefore, option A is wrong.

The owner cannot apply to the court to adjourn the proceedings as (i) there are no such proceedings and (ii) the Property is not a dwelling house. Option C is, therefore, wrong.

The Bank can choose the timing of the sale but do not need to obtain a court order for possession. Option D is, therefore, wrong.

Question 3

A solicitor acts for the owner of a freehold factory block ('the Property') subject to a mortgage (by deed) in favour of a bank ('the Bank'). The Property is currently vacant since the owner's business closed. The owner has not paid the mortgage payments for six months. The Bank believe the Property is worth £350,000 and the owner owes £370,000. The Bank would like to end the mortgage.

Which of the following is the best approach for the Bank to pursue?

A Take possession immediately with a view to redirecting income from the Property to the Bank.

B Exercise the power of sale and pursue a debt action against the owner for any shortfall.

C Pursue a debt action against the owner to recover the money owed to the Bank.

D Seek an order for foreclosure to bring the mortgage to an end and vest title in the Property in the Bank.

E Appoint a receiver to demand and receive income from the Property.

Answer

The correct option is B.

Exercise of the power of sale will end the mortgage. As the value of the Property is lower than the debt, the Bank can pursue a debt action against the owner for the difference.

Taking possession, pursuing only a debt action and appointing a receiver do not end the mortgage. Therefore, options A, C and E are wrong.

Foreclosure would end the mortgage. However, it is not in the Bank's interest to foreclose as this would extinguish the mortgage and leave the Bank with no remedy to recover any shortfall from the owner. Option D is not therefore the best answer.

6 Leases

SQE1 syllabus

This chapter will enable you to achieve the SQE1 Assessment Specification in relation to Functioning Legal Knowledge concerned with the following:

Leases

- Relationship between landlord and tenant in a lease
- Essential characteristics of a lease including the difference between a lease and a licence
- Privity of contract and privity of estate
- Rules for the passing of the benefit and burden of leasehold covenants and enforceability
- Purpose and effect of an alienation covenant
- Remedies for breach of leasehold covenants (including forfeiture)
- Different ways a lease can be terminated.

Note that for SQE1, candidates are not usually required to recall specific case names or cite statutory or regulatory authorities. Cases are provided for illustrative purposes only.

Learning outcomes

By the end of this chapter you will be able to apply relevant core legal principles and rules appropriately and effectively, at the level of a competent newly qualified solicitor in practice, to realistic client-based and ethical problems and situations in the following areas:

- The formalities required to create a lease
- The essential characteristics of a lease

- The difference between a lease and a licence
- The difference between a fixed and periodic lease and how a periodic lease can be created informally
- How covenants contained in leases may be enforced by successive owners of the freehold and leasehold estates in land
- The nature and effect of an alienation clause
- Suitable remedies for breach of covenant
- The different methods by which leases may be terminated.

6.1 Introduction

The freehold estate is an estate that endures for an uncertain length of time, whereas a leasehold estate is an estate of certain or fixed duration. A leasehold estate is 'carved' out of a freehold estate.

If a freehold owner grants a leasehold estate, the freeholder will still retain the reversion:

- The freehold estate and leasehold estate will exist concurrently in the same parcel of land.
- The freehold owner can grant a lease for as long as they like.
- A tenant (the owner of the leasehold estate) can only grant a sublease for a shorter term than the term held by the tenant.

A lease may be created for a number of reasons including for the freehold owner to:

(a) obtain income;

(b) retain an interest in the property that can be sold; and/or

(c) enforce positive covenants against a successor in title to the original tenant.

The landlord retains a fee simple absolute in possession (or freehold) as the meaning of possession in s 205 LPA 1925 extends to being in receipt of rent or profits.

Section 1(5) LPA 1925 provides that a legal estate may exist concurrently with, or subject to, another legal estate. The landlord therefore holds a reversion which entitles them to:

(a) receive the payment of rent (or profits); and

(b) retake physical possession once the lease ends.

6.2 Is a lease capable of being legal?

A lease is capable of being a legal estate in land – s 1(1)(b) LPA 1925 – a term of years absolute in possession.

6.3 Formalities

The relevant formality depends on the length of the lease.

6.3.1 Leases for more than three years

A deed is required to create a legal lease – s 52 LPA 1925. A deed must meet the criteria set out in s 1 LPMPA 1989. See **1.10.1**.

6.3.2 Leases for three years or less

Certain short-term leases require no formalities for creation. These are called 'parol leases' and can be created orally. In order to be legal, such leases must meet the criteria set out in s 54(2) LPA 1925 as follows:

(a) The lease must be for three years or less. This would include periodic leases where the period of the lease is for three years or less. For example, a monthly periodic lease.

(b) The lease must take effect in possession. This means that the tenant must have the immediate right to possess and enjoy the land.

(c) The tenant must pay the best rent which can be reasonably obtained. This means market rent.

(d) The landlord must not charge a fine or premium. This is a one-off capital sum. For example, granting the lease for £5,000. This premium could be paid instead of rent, or in addition to it.

Note that leases for three years or less can also be created by deed (see **6.3.1**).

6.3.3 When equity may intervene

Where the correct formalities for the creation of a legal lease have not been followed, equity may intervene to recognise an equitable lease. This can occur in two situations:

- where there is a contract to create or transfer a legal estate; or
- where there is an attempt to use a deed but the deed is not valid.

By contract to create or transfer a legal estate

A valid contract, complying with s 2 LPMPA 1989, is required. In addition, the remedy of specific performance of the contract must be available.

Specific performance is an equitable remedy, therefore the courts will only grant it if the person seeking it has behaved justly and fairly. This is based on the equitable maxim: 'He who seeks equity must do so with clean hands.' This means that the person seeking the remedy must not be in breach of the terms of the contract.

For equity to recognise the arrangement there must be:

- a contract;
- complying with s 2 LPMPA 1989; and
- clean hands.

This is known as the doctrine in *Walsh v Lonsdale* (1882) 21 Ch D 9. The parties had made a valid contract for a seven-year lease and the tenant had taken possession of the property. The parties omitted to execute a deed in order to create a legal lease. The court recognised an equitable lease based on the existence of the contract and the availability of specific performance. The decision was based on the equitable maxim of 'equity regards as done that which ought to be done'.

In *Coatsworth v Johnson* [1886–90] All ER Rep 547 there was a valid contract for a lease of a farm but the lease was not completed by deed and therefore could not be legal. Coatsworth took possession of the farm but breached a term of the contract. The court would not recognise the equitable lease as a consequence of Coatsworth breaching the terms of the contract and therefore not having clean hands.

However, a contract to transfer an existing legal estate (freehold or a lease) will create an equitable right known as an 'estate contract'. (See **Glossary**.)

By trying to grant a legal estate or interest but failing to use a valid deed

In this instance the parties do not deliberately enter a contract. They intend, but fail, to create a valid deed and the court finds a contract so that the transaction does not fail entirely. For this type of equitable property right to arise, there must be:

- a contract;
- complying with s 2 LPMPA 1989; and
- clean hands

In *Parker v Taswell* (1858) 119 ER 230 the parties had intended to grant a legal lease but the document had not been executed correctly and was not a deed. Therefore, it could not create a legal lease. The document did satisfy the requirements for a contract and specific performance was available therefore the document created an equitable lease.

Example 6.1

James is the freehold owner of a shop. James grants a lease for five years to Helen by deed. Helen realises that James' signature was not witnessed on the deed.

Is this a legal or equitable lease?

Comment

A lease is capable of being legal (s 1(1)(b) LPA 1925). It must be created by deed (s 52 LPA 1925) and comply with the requirements for a deed (set out in s 1 LPMPA 1989). Here, James' signature has not been witnessed so this is not a deed.

The parol lease exception does not apply as the lease is for more than three years.

Equity may intervene and recognise the arrangement as an equitable lease if there is:

- a contract;
- complying with s 2 LPMPA; and
- clean hands.

The lease document is in writing and signed and likely to contain all the expressly agreed terms, so complies with s 2 LPMPA 1989. There is nothing in the facts to suggest that Helen does not have clean hands.

An equitable lease has been created.

6.4 Essential characteristics of a lease

There are three essential requirements:

1. The estate must be for a duration permitted for a leasehold estate.
2. The grant must give exclusive possession.
3. The grant must have the correct formalities (see **6.3** above).

The court will consider the substance of any agreement and not simply its form. When the above three requirements are met, a lease has been created (even if the agreement is labelled a licence) - *Street v Mountford* [1985] 1 AC 809.

If one or more of the essential characteristics of a lease are missing, then all that has been created is a licence. The key differences between a lease and a licence are:

Lease	**Licence**
Creates a proprietary right in land that can bind a purchaser of the reversion (eg freehold estate).	Creates only a personal right (permission) that will not bind the purchaser of the reversion (eg freehold estate).
A lease can be assigned to a new tenant (ie bought and sold) and the lease continues to exist.	A licence cannot be assigned and a new licence is required if the identity of the parties to the licence changes.
An occupier with the benefit of a lease may benefit from a range of statutory protections.	Licensees in occupation do not benefit from statutory protection.

6.4.1 Permitted duration

A lease must have a definable beginning and a definable end. This is described as a fixed ascertainable period.

The lease may be for a fixed term or periodic (see **6.4.5** below).

A lease 'for the duration' (meaning the duration of the Second World War) was not a valid lease as the duration was not fixed (*Lace v Chantler* [1944] 1 All ER 305).

A lease stated to continue until the land was required by the council for road widening was not a valid fixed-term lease. It was therefore void (*Prudential Assurance v London Residuary Body* [1992] 2 AC 386).

Any attempt to create a lease for life will create a lease for a term of 90 years which ends on the death of the tenant (or as otherwise provided for in the agreement) (s 49(6) LPA 1925).

However, there is no difficulty in creating a fixed-term lease with a contractual right to bring it to a premature end. This is called a break clause. For example, a lease for 10 years with a break clause in favour of the tenant in the fifth year of the lease. The lease has a fixed ascertainable period, notwithstanding the break clause, and therefore complies with the rule.

6.4.2 Exclusive possession

A grant of anything less than exclusive possession will not create a leasehold estate. It will create a licence.

Exclusive possession is the ability for the tenant to exercise control over the land:

(i) the tenant may exclude all (including the landlord) from the land; and

(ii) exclusive possession extends beyond mere exclusive occupation. The latter is the characteristic of a licence. A tenant does not need to be in occupation to enjoy exclusive possession.

A statement that exclusive possession is not given does not prevent there being a lease if that is the true effect. If the occupier has been given general control of the property, then there is exclusive possession.

6.4.3 Lease vs licence

If there is no exclusive possession, then there can only be a licence. Often, the landowner wishes to deny exclusive possession to ensure that the occupier does not obtain the benefits of a lease (particularly security of tenure):

The landowner retains control

The landowner retaining a key does not negate exclusive possession. However, if the occupier lacks general control there will be no exclusive possession.

Hull Corporation owned a dry dock and allowed ship owners to use it to repair their ships. Despite use of the word let, the agreement was held to be a licence. This was because the ship owners lacked general control of the dock and therefore there was no exclusive possession (*Wells v Kingston upon Hull* (1875) LR 10 CP 402).

In *Westminster City Council v Clarke* [1992] 2 AC 288, the council placed Mr Clarke in a hostel room for homeless single men pursuant to an agreement entitled 'Licence to Occupy'. The licence included the following terms:

- It was expressed to be personal to Mr Clarke.
- It was not intended to create exclusive possession of any room.
- Mr Clarke's room could be changed without notice.
- Mr Clarke could be required to share the accommodation.
- Mr Clarke was not allowed to invite friends to the accommodation.
- The council's employees could enter at any time.

The council had imposed the conditions on occupancy for the harmonious occupation of the hostel. The effect of the conditions was that the council had legitimately and effectively retained for itself possession of the room occupied by Mr Clarke. He was, therefore, only a licensee.

Service occupancies

If an employer allows an employee to live in the employer's accommodation which is essential for the better performance of their duties, this will create a licence. Such a service occupancy will terminate when the employment comes to an end. This type of arrangement is relevant, for example, for caretakers and members of the police and armed forces.

Flat sharing agreements

AG Securities v Vaughan and *Antoniades v Villiers* were reported together at [1990] 1 AC 417. In both cases, each occupier had signed a single agreement described as a licence.

In *AG Securities v Vaughan* the court held that the agreements entered into by the occupiers were independent and did not confer a right of exclusive occupation on any one party. The agreements had different dates and referred to different rents. The four bedrooms in the flat were occupied on a rolling basis by incoming occupiers. The parties did not enjoy exclusive possession of the flat jointly under the terms of their agreements. As a result, the occupiers only had licence agreements.

In *Antoniades v Villiers* the court held that the agreements were interdependent and had to be read together as a single agreement. The agreements were in identical terms and signed on the same day. The court focused on the realities of the situation and found a clear intention that the occupiers (a couple) were to share a bedsit with one double bed. The intention was for the couple to acquire joint and exclusive occupation of the flat. The provision in the document allowing the owner, his agents or invitees to share occupation was held to be a sham on the basis that no-one would expect the right to be exercised. Accordingly, a lease had been created.

6.4.4 Payment of rent?

The payment of rent is not an essential characteristic of a lease. However, payment of rent supports the view that the parties intended a formal relationship of landlord and tenant (rather than an informal family or friendship relationship – *Ashburn Anstalt v Arnold* [1989] Ch 1).

6.4.5 Types of leases

<u>Fixed-term leases</u>

A fixed-term lease is essentially a contract that gives the tenant the right to occupy the premises for a certain fixed period of time. This is usually in return for an undertaking to pay the landlord a rent and to fulfil certain other obligations.

The term can be for any duration, ie one day, six months, 10 years or 99 years.

<u>Periodic leases</u>

These are often described as a 'periodic tenancy'.

A periodic lease runs from period to period until it is terminated by notice by either party. It is regarded as being a tenancy for each individual period and is, therefore, for a defined term.

Each time a period expires, the term is automatically renewed. The length of the period is determined by reference to the period for which the rent is expressed to be reserved. So, if the rent is expressed be paid monthly, then it is a monthly periodic tenancy.

Legal periodic leases can arise due to the actions of the parties when it can be inferred that the parties intended to create a lease. Where the period of the lease is for three years or less, the lease will be legal if it meets the criteria in s 54(2) LPA 1925 for a parol lease. (See **6.3.2**.)

Example 6.2

Katie is the freehold owner of 32 Mabel Grove ('the Property'). Katie allows Sally into occupation of the Property and Sally pays a rent of £600 per calendar month. Sally has now been in occupation for five years.

Has a legal lease been created?

Comment

There is a fixed ascertainable period. This is the period of a month which is a fixed period. This is because the rent is expressed to be paid monthly.

There is nothing in the facts to indicate that Sally does not have exclusive possession.

A lease is capable of being legal and would normally require a deed for its creation. However, the term of the lease is calculated by reference to the period for which the rent is expressed to be reserved. The rent is expressed to be paid monthly and therefore the period is a month (despite Sally being in occupation for five years).

The lease is a parol lease as it is for three years or less (a month), in possession (Sally took possession immediately), at the best rent reasonably obtainable (provided £600 per month is the market rent) and there is no fine or premium (there is nothing in the facts to suggest this) - s 54(2) LPA 1925.

Although rent is not an essential characteristic of a lease, payment of the monthly rent evidences an intention to create legal relations.

Sally has the benefit of a legal monthly periodic tenancy.

6.5 Relationship between a landlord and tenant in a lease

A lease is essentially a contract which creates an estate in land. It represents the agreement between the landlord and the tenant, detailing their respective rights and obligations during the term. The contractual terms contained in a lease are known as covenants.

Lease covenants are agreed through negotiation between the landlord and the tenant (or more usually their solicitors).

6.5.1 Key lease covenants

Tenant's covenants:

- rent
- contribution to insurance
- repair
- alterations
- alienation.

Landlord's covenants:

- quiet enjoyment
- insurance.

In the absence of an express obligation, certain covenants will be implied on the part of the landlord to include:

- quiet enjoyment; and
- obligations in respect of fitness of the property.

Quiet enjoyment

This means that the tenant's lawful possession of the land will not be substantially interfered with by acts of the landlord. It does not mean the absence of noise, although regular excessive noise may amount to a substantial interference.

A residential tenant is further protected by the Protection from Eviction Act (PEA) 1977 which prevents a landlord from unlawfully depriving the tenant of their occupation. Any acts likely to interfere with the residential tenant's peace or comfort that are done with the intention of causing them to give up occupation are an offence under the PEA 1977.

Obligations in respect of fitness of the property

In relation to a dwelling-house, s 11 of the Landlord and Tenant Act 1985 obliges the landlord to:

(a) keep in repair the structure and exterior of the dwelling-house;

(b) keep in repair and proper working order the installations for the supply of water, gas, electricity and sanitation; and

(c) keep in repair and proper working order the installations for space heating and water heating.

However, the landlord is only liable if there is disrepair and only once such disrepair has been notified to them.

6.5.2 The tenant's alienation covenant – an assignment or a sublease?

Alienation simply means disposal of the existing (and remaining) leasehold estate by the tenant.

Assignment

The tenant passes all of their interest under the lease to a new tenant and steps out of the picture. The new tenant steps into the shoes of the old tenant.

No new lease is created. The existing lease simply changes hands.

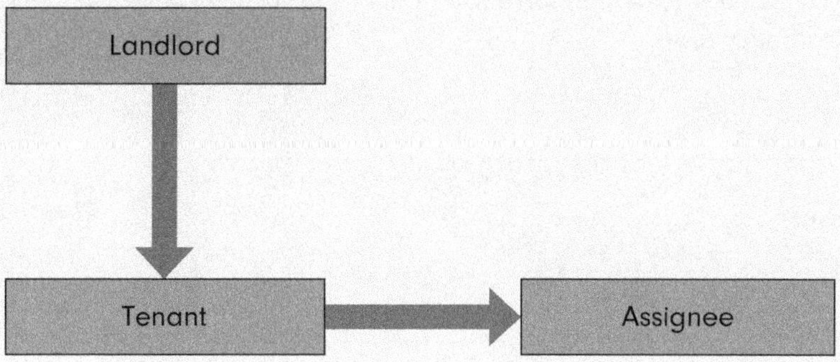

Sublease

A lesser estate is carved out of the superior estate. A new lease is created. This must be for a shorter duration than the head lease.

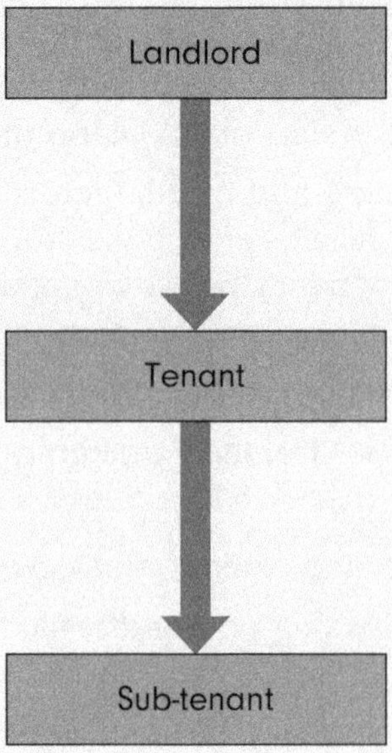

Example 6.3

Look at the figure above.

Comment

The landlord (the freehold owner) grants the head lease to the tenant for a term of 99 years. In turn, the tenant grants the sublease to the subtenant for a term of 20 years.

The tenant pays rent to the landlord. The subtenant pays rent to the tenant. The tenant has a dual capacity as:

- the tenant of the head lease; and
- the landlord of the sublease.

The three legal estates exist concurrently in relation to the same property; the freehold, the head lease and sublease.

6.5.3 Alienation

Alienation means the tenant disposing of the lease by way of:

- assignment;
- sub-lease;
- mortgage/charge;
- parting with possession/occupation.

An assignment is where the tenant passes all of their (remaining) interest in the lease to a new tenant (the assignee). No new lease is created.

The parties to a lease have contractual freedom in relation to what is permitted. However, legislation has an effect on how lease provisions are interpreted. This depends upon the nature of the alienation covenant:

(a) The open contract position – if the lease does not contain a covenant against alienation the tenant has complete freedom to deal with the lease as they wish.

(b) Absolute prohibition – there is a covenant by the tenant not to deal with the lease. This could relate to assignment or any other form of alienation.

(c) **Qualified covenant –** the covenant by the tenant is not to assign (or otherwise deal with) the lease without the landlord's consent.

(d) **Fully qualified covenant –** the tenant covenants not to assign (or otherwise deal with) the lease without the landlord's consent – such consent, not to be unreasonably withheld.

6.5.4 The effect of legislation on alienation covenants

Section 19 of the Landlord and Tenant Act (LTA) 1927 translates any qualified covenant (against assignment, underletting, charging or parting with possession) into a fully qualified covenant so that the landlord cannot unreasonably withhold consent. This does not alter an absolute prohibition.

The Landlord and Tenant Act (LTA) 1988 imposes obligations on the landlord (in relation to a qualified covenant) where the landlord has received a written application:

- to give consent (unless it is reasonable not to do so);
- to give written notice of their decision including any conditions; and
- where consent is withheld, written reasons for refusal.

This relates to any assignment, underletting, charging or parting with possession. The landlord cannot, therefore, unreasonably delay giving consent. Both these provisions relate to old and new leases.

Section 19(1A) of the LTA 1927 (originally s 22 Landlord and Tenant (Covenants) Act (LT(C)A) 1995) enables the original landlord and original tenant of a non-residential lease (granted post 1 January 1996) to agree in advance (at the point of drafting the lease) on the:

- circumstances in which the landlord may withhold its consent to an assignment; and
- conditions subject to which any consent to assign will be subject.

The circumstances and conditions are not subject to the reasonableness test set out in the LTA 1988. The most popular condition is for the former tenant to provide the landlord with an authorised guarantee agreement (AGA) as a condition of the landlord giving its consent to any assignment.

Example 6.4

In 2018, Leonard (the freehold owner) granted a 25-year commercial lease to Nicole. The lease contained:

- *a covenant by the tenant not to assign the lease without the landlord's consent; and*
- *a requirement for the tenant to provide an AGA as a condition of the landlord giving their consent to any assignment.*

Nicole wishes to assign the lease to Donna.

Can Leonard withhold his consent?

Comment

The qualified alienation covenant is translated into a fully qualified covenant so that Leonard cannot unreasonably withhold or delay his consent to the assignment (s 19 LTA 1927).

As the lease was granted post 1 January 1996 and contains both a covenant against alienation and a condition under s 19(1A) LTA 1927 Leonard is entitled to seek an AGA from Nicole as a condition of giving his consent to the assignment to Donna. Such a request is not subject to the reasonableness test.

6.6 Rules governing how covenants in leases are enforced

There are two sets of rules governing how covenants in leases are enforced. Which set of rules applies depends on when the lease was created (not assigned):

- leases created before 1 January 1996 ('Old leases'); and
- leases created after 1 January 1996 ('New leases').

The LT(C)A 1995 also includes some provisions which apply retrospectively to old leases.

6.6.1 Old leases (granted before 1996)

(a) Liability of the original tenant

There is a relationship of privity of contract between the original landlord and the original tenant. Within the lease the parties may have covenanted on behalf of themselves and their successors in title. However, even if this is not expressed within the lease, the continuing obligations will be implied under s 79 LPA 1925.

If the original tenant (T1) assigns the lease to T2:

- T1 remains subject to the burden of the covenants in the lease;
- but ceases to be entitled to the benefit of covenants in the lease.

T1's contractual liability lasts for the duration of the lease.

(b) Liability of an assignee

When the original tenant (T1) assigns the lease to an assignee (T2) there is a relationship of privity of estate between the landlord and T2. Privity of estate always exists between a current landlord and current tenant. This means the tenant is entitled to exclusive possession, liable to pay rent and is the party in whom the lease is currently vested (*Spencer's Case* (1583) 5 Co Rep 16a).

T2 is liable for breaches of all real covenants. These are covenants which touch and concern the land and include both positive and restrictive covenants. The test created in *P & A Swift Investments v Combined English Stores Group plc* [1989] AC 632 can be used:

(i) a 'touching and concerning' covenant must benefit only the dominant owner for the time being, so that, if separated from their land, it ceases to be advantageous to them;

(ii) the covenant must affect the nature, quality, mode of user or value of the land of the dominant owner; and

(iii) the covenant must not be expressed to be personal (ie must not have been given only to one specific dominant owner).

Examples of real covenants include covenants:

- to pay rent, rates or taxes;
- to repair;
- relating to the use of the property.

A purely personal obligation would not be a real covenant. For example, a promise by T1 to give the landlord a single red rose on the first day of each month.

An assignee is only liable under privity of estate for the duration that the lease is vested in them (ie whilst they are the tenant in occupation and paying rent). However, it is common for a landlord to insist that each assignee covenants directly with them to observe and perform the covenants contained in the lease. This creates a relationship of privity of contract between the landlord and all of the assignees (and not simply between the original landlord and the original tenant). For the purposes of this chapter, it will be assumed that no such direct covenant is obtained.

(c) **What if T2 fails to comply with an obligation?**

If T2 defaults the landlord has a choice; they can pursue:

- T1 via privity of contract;
- T2 via privity of estate; or
- both of them.

Example 6.5

In 1994, Loretta, the freehold owner, granted a 50-year lease to Toby (by deed). In 2010, Toby assigned the lease to Alison (by deed and with Loretta's consent). Last year, Alison assigned the lease to Gwen (by deed and with Loretta's consent). Gwen has failed to comply with the covenants in the lease.

Who is liable?

Comment

The lease was created in 1994 and is therefore an old lease.

Toby remains bound by privity of contract, as the original contracting tenant, either as a consequence of an express covenant or by virtue of s 79 LPA 1925.

Gwen is bound by privity of estate as the lease is currently vested in her. The covenant to pay rent is a real covenant.

Loretta can take action against Toby, Gwen or both of them.

(d) **Recovery between tenants**

If the original tenant is sued as a result of a breach which they did not commit they can either take action:

(i) At common law against the tenant in possession at the time of the breach (ie the current tenant) - *Moule v Garrett* (1872) LR Ex 101. Where one person discharges the liability of another, that person may seek to recover the amount they have paid from the person whose liability they have discharged; or

(ii) On the indemnity covenant (contained in the deed of assignment) against the person to whom they assigned the lease. Most assignments contain an express indemnity covenant; or

(iii) In the absence of an express indemnity covenant, this will be implied into any assignment for value by s 77 LPA 1925 (unregistered title) and Sch 12, para 20 Land Registration Act 2002 (registered title). The indemnity is a promise by the assignee to the assignor to observe and perform the tenant's covenants and make good any damage caused by any future breach.

(e) **Sale (or assignment) of the reversion**

On a sale of the reversion, the benefits and burdens of the landlord's covenants which touch and concern the land are transmitted to the new landlord - ss 141 and 142 LPA 1925 respectively. This enables the new landlord to pursue either the original tenant (via privity of contract) or the current tenant (via privity of estate).

The new landlord only has the benefit and burden of the covenants whilst the reversion is vested in them.

Example 6.6

Kamal was the freehold owner of 64 Grange Road ('the Property'). In 1995, Kamal granted Tina a 50-year lease of the Property (by deed). The lease contained:

- *a covenant by Tina to only use the Property as a hairdresser; and*
- *a covenant by Kamal to maintain the Property in repair.*

In 2018, Tina assigned the lease (by deed and with Kamal's consent) to Amy. In 2022, Kamal sold the freehold reversion to Laurie. Amy is now using the Property as a sweet shop and there is a large hole in the roof of the Property.

What action can be taken by whom and against whom in respect of the breaches of covenant relating to the Property?

Comment

Laurie will have the benefit of the landlord's covenants that touch and concern the land. A covenant relating to the use of the Property touches and concerns the land.

As the original tenant, Tina is bound by the user covenant throughout the term of the lease. Laurie can pursue Tina via privity of contract (as the benefit of the covenant has passed to Laurie via s 141 LPA 1925).

Laurie can also pursue Amy via privity of estate as the burden of the covenant has passed to Amy (*Spencer's Case*) and Laurie has the benefit of the covenant (s 141 LPA 1925).

The covenant by Kamal to keep the Property in repair touches and concerns the land. The benefit of the covenant passes to Amy (via privity of estate) and the burden of the covenant passes to Laurie via s 142 LPA 1925. There is a relationship of privity of estate between Laurie and Amy as they are in the direct relationship of landlord and tenant. Amy can therefore seek a remedy from Laurie.

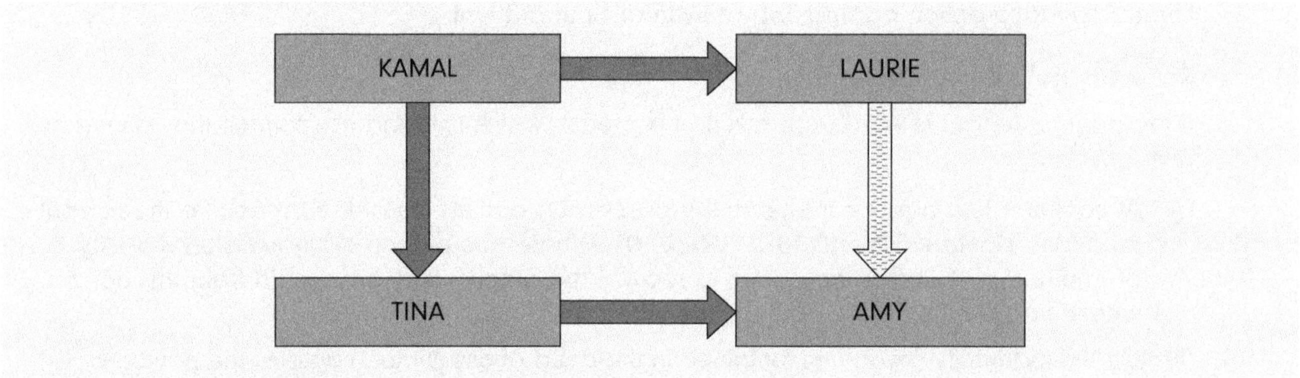

6.6.2 New leases (granted after 1996)

The LT(C)A 1995 applies to all leases granted after 1 January 1996. The LT(C)A 1995 replaces the existing law of privity of contract and privity of estate with a new set of statutory rules.

(a) The position of the tenant

The tenant (meaning the original tenant and any subsequent assignee) is bound by the covenants of the lease only whilst the lease is vested in them. Upon an assignment of the lease, all the landlord and tenant covenants pass to the assignee unless they are expressed to be personal – s 3 LT(C)A 1995. An assignee takes the burden of the tenant covenants and acquires the benefit of the landlord covenants.

The covenants do not need to touch and concern the land. Only those covenants expressed to be personal do not pass to the assignee.

The assigning tenant is automatically released from any liability under the lease. They cease to be bound by the lease covenants (and cease to be entitled to the benefit of any landlord covenants) – s 5 LT(C)A 1995.

If the assignee breaches a covenant in the lease, the landlord can only pursue the assignee (ie the current tenant).

(b) **The position of the landlord**

Upon a sale of the reversion, the new landlord takes the burden of the landlord covenants and acquires the benefit of the tenant covenants, provided that the covenants were not expressed to be personal - s 3 LT(C)A 1995.

The covenants do not need to touch and concern the land. Only those covenants expressed to be personal do not pass to the new landlord.

The outgoing landlord is not automatically released following an assignment of the reversion. The outgoing landlord has to follow the criteria in ss 6 and 8 LT(C)A 1995 in order to obtain a release from the landlord covenants. If a release is not obtained, the outgoing landlord remains liable on the landlord covenants.

This means that (if the outgoing landlord has not been released) the tenant will have a choice of pursuing the former landlord, the new landlord or both.

The decision in *Avonridge Property Co Ltd v Mashru* [2005] UKHL 70 provides an alternative exit route for landlords. The landlord can limit their liability by stating in the lease that their liability ends once they have disposed of the reversion. The landlord is, therefore, only responsible for the landlord's covenants whilst they hold the reversion.

6.6.3 Authorised Guarantee Agreements

(a) **What is an Authorised Guarantee Agreement (AGA)?**

The effect of s 5 of the LT(C)A 1995 is to release the outgoing tenant (ie the original or any subsequent tenant) from any liability under the lease upon assignment. Accordingly, the landlord cannot pursue the former tenant. The landlord may be able to improve their position by asking the outgoing tenant to enter into an AGA - s 16 LT(C)A 1995.

An AGA is an agreement between the landlord and the outgoing tenant under which the outgoing (or former) tenant guarantees that the assignee (incoming tenant) will perform the lease covenants. The former tenant gives the AGA to the landlord, which effectively means, if the assignee (incoming tenant) does not perform the lease covenants, the landlord can take action against the former (outgoing) tenant who has given an AGA.

(b) **Terms of the AGA**

The obligation under an AGA is a primary obligation. This means that the landlord may pursue the former tenant without taking any action against the assignee.

An AGA only requires the former tenant to guarantee their immediate assignee. Therefore, if the assignee assigns the lease, the AGA ceases to be of effect (s 16(4) LT(C)A 1995) which means the former tenant no longer has liability for the tenant covenants. Only one former tenant can be liable under an AGA at any one time.

The landlord can, however, require the former tenant to enter a new lease if the assignee is declared bankrupt and the lease is disclaimed by the trustee in bankruptcy.

(c) **When can a landlord require an AGA?**

A landlord can only seek an AGA where:

- the lease contains a covenant against alienation without the landlord's consent (ie the tenant cannot sell the lease without first asking the landlord's permission); and
- it is either reasonable to do so or, in the case of a commercial lease, it is a condition of the landlord giving its consent (under s 19(1A) LTA 1927). (See **6.5.4**.)

Example 6.7

In 2010, Lucy, the freehold owner, granted a lease (by deed) to Tanveer for a term of 20 years at an annual rent of £33,000. In 2015, Tanveer assigned the lease to Ashleigh. In 2016, Lucy assigned the freehold reversion to Freddie. Last year, Ashleigh assigned the lease to Gabriel. Gabriel has not paid the rent since the date of the assignment to him.

Who can Freddie recover the rent from?

Comment

The benefit and burden of all landlord and tenant covenants pass to Freddie on the assignment to him of the freehold reversion and to Gabriel on the assignment of the lease - s 3 LT(C)A 1995. This means that Freddie can pursue Gabriel for payment of the rent.

Ashleigh was automatically released from his liability under the lease when he assigned it to Gabriel - s 5 LT(C)A 1995.

Ashleigh may have given an AGA when he assigned the lease - s 16 LT(C)A 1995. If so, Freddie can pursue Ashleigh for the unpaid rent as Freddie will have the benefit of the AGA under s 3 LT(C)A 1995.

Tanveer was automatically released from his liability under the lease when he assigned it to Ashleigh (s 5 LT(C)A 1995). If Tanveer provided an AGA, it would cease to have any effect upon the assignment by Ashleigh as an AGA only guarantees performance by the immediate assignee - s 16(4) LT(C)A 1995.

Freddie can pursue the current tenant, the former tenant (if an AGA was provided) or both of them.

(d) **Recovery between the tenants**

A former tenant who suffers loss due to liability under an AGA as a consequence of the default of the assignee may:

- recover from the assignee on the basis of the principle in *Moule v Garrett* (see **6.6.1(d)**); or
- more commonly, on the basis of an express indemnity given by the immediate assignee.

Unlike old leases, indemnity covenants are not implied on every assignment - s 14 LT(C)A 1995.

In addition (or as an alternative) to an AGA, a landlord can seek a contractual guarantor to guarantee the performance of an assignee. This is a complex area of law which is beyond the scope of this manual.

6.6.4 Retrospective effect of the Landlord and Tenant (Covenants) Act 1995

Sections 17, 18 and 19 apply to both old and new leases. The aim of this retrospective effect is to improve the position of a former tenant who remains liable either due to:

- privity of contract in an old lease; or
- the terms of an AGA if a new lease.

Section 17

This relates to the recovery of a fixed charge from a former tenant. A fixed charge includes rent. Before the landlord can pursue a former tenant for the payment of rent, they must:

- serve a default notice;
- on the former tenant;
- within six calendar months of the fixed charge falling due.

If the landlord fails to serve the default notice, they cannot recover the fixed charge from the former tenant. If the former tenant pays the sum demanded in *full*, the former tenant can request an overriding lease from the landlord (see s 19 LT(C)A 1995 below).

The s 17 default notice acts as an early warning to the former tenant and ensures that the landlord cannot allow arrears of rent to accumulate before taking action.

For the landlord, the s 17 default notice is an additional bureaucratic hurdle that must be completed before the landlord can take action against a former tenant.

Example 6.8

In 1995, Liam (the freehold owner) granted a lease (by deed) for a term of 35 years to Tahir. Tahir covenanted to pay rent of £6,000 per year by equal payments in advance on the first day of each month. In 2020, Tahir assigned the lease to Amber (by deed and with Liam's consent). Amber has paid no rent for the last year.

Who can Liam pursue for the unpaid rent?

Comment

The lease was created before 1 January 1996 and is, therefore, an old lease governed by the rules of privity of estate and contract.

As an assignee, Amber is bound by privity of estate to observe real covenants. The covenant to pay rent touches and concerns the land. However, as Amber has not paid the rent for a year it may not be worth pursuing her.

Tahir is the original tenant and is bound by privity of contract either as a consequence of an express covenant or implied by s 79 LPA 1925. Tahir remains bound throughout the duration of the lease.

Before Liam can take action against Tahir for the outstanding rent, Liam must first serve on Tahir a default notice under s 17 LT(C)A 1995 within six calendar months of the fixed charge falling due. As Amber has not paid the rent for a year, Liam would only be able to recover the most recent six months' rent from Tahir.

Remember, s 17 has retrospective effect and applies to both old and new leases.

Section 18

This section applies where an assignee agrees to a variation of the terms of the lease which was not contemplated in the original lease.

Section 19

If a former tenant pays the sum demanded in accordance with a s 17 default notice in full, s 19 allows the former tenant to request an overriding lease from the landlord. An overriding lease is:

- the same duration as the original lease but less three days;
- on the same terms as the original lease; and
- granted by the landlord to the former tenant.

The former tenant becomes the landlord to the defaulting assignee, but is obliged to pay rent to the landlord and comply with the tenant covenants in the same way as the original lease.

Example 6.9

In 2018, Lionel (the freehold owner) granted a lease (by deed) to Tansy for a term of 25 years at an annual rent of £12,000 payable in advance by equal monthly payments on the first day of each month. In 2022, Tansy assigned the lease (by deed and with Lionel's consent) to Annalise. Annalise has not paid the rent for the last seven months.

Can Lionel take action against Tansy for the unpaid rent?

Comment

Tansy was automatically released from any liability under the lease when she assigned to Annalise - s 5 LT(C)A 1995.

Tansy will only be liable for the rent if, when she assigned the lease, she provided an AGA to Lionel - s 16 LT(C)A 1995. If so, Lionel must first serve a default notice on Tansy within six calendar months of the fixed charge falling due - s 17 LT(C)A 1995.

The rent has not been paid for seven months. Lionel cannot claim the month's rent due seven months ago, but can claim the remaining six months provided he serves the default notice immediately.

If Tansy pays the sum demanded in full, she can request an overriding lease from Lionel - s 19 LT(C)A 1995.

6.7 Landlord's remedies for non-payment of rent

The landlord has a number of remedies available for non-payment of rent as follows:

- debt action
- commercial rent arrears recovery
- forfeiture.

6.7.1 Debt action

A lease is likely to contain an express covenant by the tenant to pay rent. In the absence of such an express obligation, for example, in the case of a parol lease, such an obligation is implied.

The landlord may sue the tenant for debt. This is not a damages claim and it does not bring the lease to an end.

The landlord may pursue the current tenant, a former tenant (via privity of contract or an AGA) or both. In relation to a former tenant, the landlord will need to serve a default notice under s 17 LT(C)A 1995. (See **6.6.4**.)

The landlord is prevented, by s 19 of the Limitation Act 1980, from bringing such a claim after the expiration of six years from the date on which the arrears became due.

Pursuing an action in debt acknowledges the existence of the lease and has the potential to waive the right for the landlord to forfeit (see **6.7.3**).

6.7.2 Commercial rent arrears recovery (CRAR)

CRAR was introduced by the Tribunal, Courts and Enforcement Act 2007 and came into effect in April 2014. It abolished the previous rules in relation to distress.

CRAR is only available against the tenant in possession (ie the tenant currently responsible for paying the rent). It consists of the landlord entering the premises in order to seize the tenant's goods and sell them. The arrears of rent are paid off from the proceeds of sale. A court order is not required but there is a procedure to follow. CRAR:

- applies to leases of commercial property only;
- can only be used to recover 'normal' rent (ie not service charge or insurance premiums even if the lease states these other payments are reserved at rent);
- the rent due must exceed a minimum of seven days' rent;

- the landlord must give the tenant a minimum of seven days' notice of their intention to take control of the tenant's goods. Such notice must be given by an authorised enforcement agent (formerly a bailiff). The tenant's goods are 'bound' (ie controlled by the landlord) at the date of the notice. The tenant may challenge the landlord's warning notice in court; and
- only an enforcement agent may take control of the tenant's goods.

CRAR does not bring the lease to an end. Exercising CRAR acknowledges the existence of the lease and may therefore waive the landlord's right to forfeit (see **6.7.3**).

6.7.3 Forfeiture

Forfeiture for non-payment of rent:

- is also known as the right to re-enter - see s 1(2)(e) LPA 1925;
- can only be exercised against the tenant in possession (not a former tenant);
- is the right for a landlord to retake physical possession of the premises thereby prematurely terminating the lease.

The right to forfeit must be expressly reserved by the lease. This is commonly called a 'forfeiture clause'. Most professionally drawn-up leases include such a clause. An example of a standard form of forfeiture clause is set out below:

> PROVIDED ALWAYS and it is hereby agreed that if the said rent or any part thereof shall be unpaid for 21 days after becoming duly payable (*whether or not the same shall have been formally demanded*) or if the Tenant shall fail to perform her covenants or obligations hereunder then in any of the said cases it shall be lawful for the Landlord or any person duly authorised by the Landlord in that behalf to re-enter the Premises or any part thereof in the name of the whole and thereupon this demise shall absolutely determine but without prejudice to any right of action of the Landlord in respect of any breach of the Tenant's covenants herein contained.

Waiver

Once the right to forfeit has arisen, the landlord may lose the right to forfeit in respect of *that* breach if by their conduct they are deemed to have waived it.

Waiver may be express or implied. It will be implied if the landlord does some unequivocal act showing recognition of the continued existence of the lease and in full knowledge of the facts giving them the right to forfeit. Examples of implied waiver include exercising CRAR, demanding future rent or suing for or accepting rent after the breach.

Waiver will not be implied by such conduct if the landlord has already shown that they no longer regard the lease as subsisting; for example, where the landlord has commenced possession proceedings.

Method of forfeiture

The landlord must make a formal demand for the rent due by presenting themselves at the premises on the due date for payment between sunrise and sunset unless the lease expressly exempts the landlord from this requirement. See the words in italics in the specimen forfeiture clause above.

The landlord may forfeit either by:

- peacefully re-entering the premises; or
- by suing for and obtaining a possession order in the courts.

Section 6 Criminal Law Act 1977 makes it a criminal offence to repossess any premises (residential or business) using force.

Where the premises are let wholly or partly as a dwelling and the occupier continues to reside at the premises, the landlord must obtain a court order before re-entering – s 2 PEA 1977.

Relief for the tenant

The tenant may apply to the court for relief against forfeiture. If such relief is granted, then the tenant may retake the premises on the terms of the original lease as though there had been no forfeiture.

The tenant may seek relief as follows:

(i) if the landlord sues for possession and the tenant pays all the arrears of rent and costs before the trial, the court must generally grant relief;

(ii) the tenant can also apply to the court for relief within six months of the landlord's re-entry pursuant to a court order. In this case, however, relief is at the discretion of the court; and

(iii) if the landlord forfeits a non-residential lease by re-entry without court proceedings, the six-month time limit does not apply and the court can exercise its inherent equitable jurisdiction to grant relief in such a case.

Example 6.10

In 1995, Fred (the freehold owner) granted a 40-year lease (by deed) of 21 High Street ('the Property') to Matthias subject to a rent of £24,000 payable quarterly in advance. The lease was assigned to Kay in 2015 (by deed and with Fred's consent). Kay has closed her business and has not paid the last three quarters' rent.

What remedies can Fred pursue and against whom?

Comment

This is an old lease. Fred can pursue:

- Kay via privity of estate; and
- Matthias via privity of contract.

Fred can claim an action in debt for the rent against Kay, Matthias or both. It is probably not worth pursing Kay as she has closed her business and has significant arrears.

In order to pursue Matthias, Fred must first serve a default notice within six calendar months of the fixed charge falling due. Provided a notice is immediately served, Fred may be able to recover the last two quarters' rent, but not the rent due nine months ago.

CRAR is not a viable remedy as Kay has closed her business and there is unlikely to be anything of value at the Property.

Provided that there is an express clause in the lease, Fred may forfeit the lease either by peaceful re-entry or by obtaining a court order for possession. If the Property or any part is occupied as a dwelling, then a court order must be obtained.

6.8 Landlord's remedies for breach of other covenants

The landlord has the following remedies in relation to a breach of a covenant other than the covenant to pay rent:

- Damages
- Specific performance
- Forfeiture
- Self-help remedy

6.8.1 Damages

A claim for damages does not bring the lease to an end. The ordinary contractual rules as to the measure of damages will generally apply so that damages are limited to:

(a) such as may fairly and reasonably be considered either arising naturally, ie according to the usual course of things, from such breach of contract itself; or

(b) such as may reasonably be supposed to have been in contemplation of both parties at the time they made the contract, as the probable result of the breach of it.

Damages may be claimed against the tenant in possession, a former tenant who remains liable (ie via privity of contract in an old lease or via an AGA in a new lease) or both. A default notice under s 17 LT(C)A 1995 is not required to be served on a former tenant, as damages are not included within the definition of a fixed charge.

Any claim for damages for disrepair is limited to the amount by which the reversionary interest has diminished in value as a consequence of the disrepair (s 18 LTA 1927). Where the lease has three or more years unexpired, the landlord must first serve on the tenant a s 146 LPA 1925 notice (see **6.8.3** below). Such notice must include a statement to the effect that the tenant is entitled to serve a counter notice claiming the benefit of the Leasehold Property (Repairs) Act 1938. The tenant has 28 days within which to serve a counter notice and if served, the landlord cannot take further action without leave of the court.

6.8.2 Specific performance

This is a discretionary remedy against the tenant in possession. It does not bring the lease to an end.

The remedy is rarely ordered in respect of the repairing covenant as damages will usually be an adequate remedy.

6.8.3 Forfeiture

Forfeiture for breach of covenant, other than the covenant for non-payment of rent, must be expressly reserved in the lease. If the landlord waives the breach then the landlord loses the right to forfeit for that breach.

The landlord can forfeit by peaceable re-entry or a court order for possession. If the premises are wholly or partly let as a dwelling house and the tenant is in occupation then a court order is required (s 2 PEA 1977).

Forfeiture brings the lease to an end and is exercised against the tenant in possession. Before the landlord can forfeit, they must generally serve a notice on the tenant under s 146 LPA 1925:

(a) specifying the breach;

(b) requiring it to be remedied within a reasonable time, if capable of remedy; and

(c) requiring compensation if desired.

Breach of a covenant against alienation, ie not to assign or underlet, is a once and for all breach and is not capable of remedy. The landlord, therefore, does not have to include a reasonable time within which to remedy the breach within their s 146 notice (however, relief against forfeiture may be available).

If the tenant remedies the breach within the time specified, there can be no forfeiture. If the tenant does not remedy the breach within a reasonable time after receiving the notice (assuming the breach is capable of remedy), the landlord may forfeit.

Relief against forfeiture for tenant/sub-tenant

The tenant can apply for relief against forfeiture either as part of the landlord's possession proceedings or in response to the landlord peaceably re-entering the premises (s 146(2) LPA 1925).

The court may grant relief on such terms as it thinks fit but he who seeks equity must do so with clean hands. The effect of relief is that the lease continues as before as if forfeiture had not happened.

If a head lease is forfeited, then any sublease ceases to exist. A subtenant can apply for relief against forfeiture of the head lease (s 146(4) LPA 1925), even in cases where the tenant may not be able to obtain relief. The relief here consists of the court vesting the head lease in the sub-lessee and on such terms as to rent, costs and damages as the court thinks fit.

6.8.4 Self-help remedy

There is a self-help remedy for landlords in relation to a breach of the tenant's covenant to repair (arising from *Jervis v Harris* [1996] Ch 195). The lease must contain a provision that allows the landlord to:

- enter and inspect the property;
- give the tenant notice that repair is required and a time period for the tenant to undertake the repairs;
- if the tenant does not complete the work the landlord can enter the property and do the work; and
- the landlord can recover the cost of the work as a debt due from the tenant thus: avoiding the provisions of s 18 LTA 1927 and the Leasehold Property (Repairs) Act 1938.

6.9 Tenant's remedies for breach of a landlord covenant

The tenant has the following remedies available:

- specific performance/injunction
- damages
- self-help

6.9.1 Specific performance/injunction

This is an equitable and, therefore, discretionary remedy which is rarely ordered in respect of the repairing covenant as damages will usually be an adequate remedy.

6.9.2 Damages

The ordinary contractual principles apply (see **6.8.1**).

6.9.3 Self-help

The landlord's failure to perform an obligation does not entitle the tenant to withhold the rent. However, in relation to a repair obligation, the tenant may notify the landlord that the repair is needed and that the tenant will carry out the repair if the landlord fails to do so. If the tenant then carries out the repairs, they may withhold rent until the ascertained cost of repair has been repaid. This is common law set off.

As an alternative, if the tenant does withhold payment of rent and the landlord sues the tenant, equity may allow the tenant to have their unliquidated claim set off against the liability for rent. This will only occur where the connection between the two claims is sufficiently direct so that it would be manifestly unjust not to allow set off. The tenant's claim must, therefore, be one that arises directly from the relationship of landlord and tenant created by the lease. This is equitable set off.

Most well drafted commercial leases will exclude the effect of both common law and equitable set off.

6.10 Determination of a lease

Leases can be brought to an end by a variety of differing methods, including:

- effluxion of time;
- notice to quit;
- break clause;
- surrender;
- disclaimer;
- frustration;
- repudiatory breach;
- merger; and
- forfeiture.

6.10.1 By effluxion of time

A fixed-term lease comes to an end when the term comes to an end. For example, a lease for five years granted on 1 January 2020 expires by effluxion of time on 31 December 2024.

6.10.2 Notice to quit

A periodic tenancy will continue indefinitely from one period to the next until either party gives the other notice to quit. This ability cannot be reserved to one party alone.

The general rule is that one full period's notice is required. For example, a weekly tenancy would require a week's notice and a monthly tenancy a month's notice. Such notice should expire at the end of a clear period. A yearly tenancy requires not less than a half year's notice.

If the premises are wholly or partly let as a dwelling house and the tenant is in occupation then not less than four weeks' notice must be given (s 5 PEA 1977).

6.10.3 Break clause

The landlord and tenant can agree to include a contractual break clause within the lease. This may be exercised by the landlord, the tenant or both. A break clause can be a fixed date or on a rolling basis in either case exercised by one party giving notice to the other of their desire to activate the break clause.

6.10.4 Surrender

This requires the landlord and tenant to mutually agree for the tenant's estate to be yielded up to the landlord. The lease is then merged into the reversionary estate and extinguished. An express surrender must be contained in a deed.

Surrender only terminates the lease agreed to be surrendered. It does not terminate the interest of any sub-tenant (even if the rights of the sub-tenant were unknown to the landlord).

6.10.5 Disclaimer

Disclaimer arises upon the bankruptcy/liquidation of the tenant. The trustee in bankruptcy or liquidator can disclaim contracts which given rise to a liability to pay money or perform any onerous act.

Disclaimer releases the tenant from all further liability but it does not end any sub-tenancy. A sub-tenant may seek an order to vest the disclaimed property in themselves.

6.10.6 Frustration

A contract is frustrated when something unexpected happens (through no fault of either party) which makes the performance of the contract significantly different from what was agreed. The doctrine is, in principle, applicable to leases but there are no reported cases where a lease has been held to be frustrated. It may apply where the property is destroyed or disappears.

6.10.7 Repudiatory breach

If one party to a contract commits a breach which goes to the root of the contract, the other party can accept that repudiation and regard the contract as at an end. There is limited case law to support that a lease may be terminated in such a way as a consequence of the actions by the landlord.

6.10.8 Merger

The tenant purchases the freehold reversion and holds both interests at the same time. Provided there is no contrary intention, the lease merges into the reversionary title and is extinguished.

6.10.9 Forfeiture

See **6.7.3** and **6.8.3**.

Summary

- The key differences between a freehold and a lease and the reasons a lease may be created.
- The formalities for creating a lease.
- The essential characteristics of a lease.
- The key differences between a lease and a licence.
- The difference between a fixed term lease and a periodic tenancy.
- The tenant's covenant against alienation.
- The relationship between landlord and tenant in an old lease.
- The relationship between a landlord and a tenant in a new lease.
- The retrospective effect of the LT(C)A 1995.
- Landlord's remedies for non-payment of rent.
- Landlord's remedies for breaches of covenant other than the covenant to pay rent.
- Tenant's remedies for breach of covenant.
- How leases end (determination of leases).

Sample questions

Question 1

A freehold owner grants a five-year lease to a tenant. The document creating the lease is described as a deed but the freehold owner's signature is not witnessed and the document does not contain all the terms agreed by the parties. However, the tenant immediately moved into the property and has paid the freehold owner a regular monthly rent at the market rate.

Has a legal lease been created?

A Yes, as a five-year lease can be created without any formality.

B Yes, it is a legal periodic tenancy created by parol due to exclusive possession and payment of rent.

C No, in order to be a legal lease a deed is always required.

D No, the document is not a deed but equity may recognise the agreement.

E No, it is a licence as the agreement does not contain all the expressly agreed terms.

Comment

The correct option is B.

The document creating the lease does not meet the requirements for a deed. However, certain leases do not require a deed. Therefore option C is wrong.

Equity would not intervene as the document does not contain all the expressly agreed terms. Therefore, option D is wrong.

The tenant immediately took possession and paid a monthly rent at market rent with no fine or premium, thus creating a monthly periodic tenancy. Therefore, option E is wrong and option B is correct.

A fixed term five-year lease cannot be created informally. Therefore, option A is wrong.

Question 2

In 2015, a freehold owner granted a 30-year commercial lease (by deed) to a clothes retailer. In 2017, the lease was assigned to a sweetshop. In 2020, the lease was assigned to a newsagent. In 2023, the lease was assigned to a bookseller. Each assignment was by deed and with the freehold owner's consent. The freehold owner required the provision of an authorised guarantee agreement as a condition of giving consent on each assignment. The bookseller has failed to pay the latest quarter's rent.

From whom can the freehold owner recover the outstanding rent?

A From the newsagent and the bookseller only.

B From the bookseller only.

C From the clothes retailer and the bookseller only.

D From the clothes retailer, the sweetshop, the newsagent and the bookseller.

E From the newsagent only.

Answer

The correct option is A.

The lease was created after 1 January 1996 and is, therefore, governed by the LT(C)A 1995. This means that, upon each assignment, the outgoing tenant is released from liability under the lease unless they have provided an AGA (ss 5 and 16 LT(C)A 1995). The benefit and burden of all covenants pass to the assignee (s 3).

An AGA only guarantees the immediate assignee. Upon a further assignment the AGA ceases to have effect (s 16(4) LT(C)A 1995).

The result is that the AGAs given by the clothes retailer and the sweetshop are no longer of any effect and the freehold owner can only pursue the bookseller (the current tenant) and/or the newsagent as a consequence of the AGA.

Options B, C, D and E are, therefore, wrong.

Question 3

In 1995, the freehold owner granted a commercial lease (by deed) to a company for a term of 40 years. The lease contained a repair obligation on the part of the tenant. The company quickly expanded its business and moved to larger premises and assigned the lease to a distributor in 2010. In 2021, the lease was assigned to a warehouse business. Each assignment was by deed and with the consent of the freehold owner. The property is in disrepair and the warehouse business does not have the financial resources to undertake the work. The freehold owner does not wish to bring the lease to an end as it would be hard to find a new tenant.

Which of the following provides the best advice to the freehold owner?

A Forfeit the lease and relet the property.

B Enter the property, conduct the repairs and recover the cost from the warehouse business as a debt due.

C Pursue a claim for damages for breach of repair against the distributor via privity of estate.

D Pursue a claim in damages for breach of repair against the warehouse business via privity of estate.

E Pursue a claim in damages for breach of repair against the company via privity of contract.

Answer

The correct option is E.

The freehold owner does not wish to end the lease so forfeiture is not a good option. Option A is, therefore, wrong.

The warehouse business does not have the resources to pay for the repairs so it is not sensible to pursue it either via privity of estate or a *Jervis v Harris* self-help remedy. Options B and D are, therefore, wrong.

The freehold owner can pursue a damages claim against the original tenant via privity of contract. As the business expanded, the original tenant seems a better target to recover the cost of repair. Option E is, therefore, the best answer.

The distributor was only responsible for the covenant to repair whilst the lease was vested in him. Option C is, therefore, wrong.

7 Unregistered Land

SQE1 syllabus

- Methods to protect and enforce third party interests
- Core principles of unregistered title to land:
  - role of title deeds
  - land charges
  - continuing role of doctrine of notice

Note that for SQE1, candidates are not usually required to recall specific case names or cite statutory or regulatory authorities. Cases are provided for illustrative purposes only.

Learning outcomes

By the end of this chapter you will be able to apply relevant core legal principles and rules appropriately and effectively, at the level of a competent newly qualified solicitor in practice, to realistic client-based and ethical problems and situations in the following areas:

- Understand the basics of unregistered land
- Explain and apply the rules governing enforceability of third party rights and interests in unregistered land.

7.1 Introduction

Prior to the introduction of the registered land system in 1925, unregistered land was the only system in existence. The unregistered land system was codified by the Law of Property Act (LPA) 1925 at the same time as the introduction of the Land Registration Act (LRA) 1925.

Although it was assumed that all land would be registered very promptly, it is estimated that around 12% of properties in England and Wales remain unregistered. It is therefore necessary to have an understanding of the unregistered land system.

7.2 Proof of title

When an owner of unregistered land comes to sell the land, they must prove their ownership. This is done by producing documents to show that the owner (and their predecessors in title) has uninterrupted possession of the land for 15 years (s 44 LPA 1925). The bundle of deeds and documents is called an 'epitome of title'. The epitome of title will consist of a schedule of documents with photocopies of the documents attached.

The epitome of title starts with a good root of title. This is a document which:

- shows ownership of the whole of the legal and equitable interest in the land;
- contains a recognisable description of the land;
- does not cast any doubt on the title; and
- is at least 15 years old.

Note that Land Registry made the whole of England and Wales subject to compulsory registration on 1 December 1990 (see further **8.3**) and so all good root documents will now pre-date that date. However, the theory that a good root of title must be at least 15 years old remains correct.

A good root of title will usually be a conveyance (by deed). A conveyance provides a good root of title on the assumption that title was investigated when the title was previously conveyed. So, if the seller offers the conveyance to them in 1980 as a root of title, the buyer's solicitor can assume that the seller's solicitor investigated title in 1980.

Gifts of land (including assents where the executors of an estate gift land to beneficiaries under will) do not provide such security. This is because the recipient of the gift does not investigate title.

Where an unregistered lease is being sold, the epitome of title will include the lease, plus documents showing uninterrupted possession for 15 years (or a shorter period if the lease is for a duration of less than 15 years).

Prior to exchange of contracts, the buyer must investigate title and inspect the land. In addition to checking that legal title has passed to the seller, the buyer will also carefully scrutinise the epitome of title to discover if there are any third party rights affecting the land. It is possible that a conveyance of the land to either the seller or a predecessor in title creates, for example, an easement or a restrictive covenant. Where the epitome reveals a third party right created prior to the root of title, the buyer is entitled to call for a copy of the earlier document.

Example 7.1

Mr and Mrs Smith ('the Smiths') plan to sell their house, 48 Marlin Way ('the Property'). The Property was conveyed to the Smiths in 1985. From the bundle of deeds the following is apparent:

1985	*Conveyance to the Smiths by Robert Edwards*
1974	*Conveyance to Robert Edwards by Samuel Winter*
1954	*Conveyance to Samuel Winter by Hilda Baker containing restrictive covenants.*

What is the root of title?

Comment

The 1985 conveyance is a good root of title. However, the buyer is entitled to call for a copy of the 1954 conveyance as it contains reference to pre-root third party rights. The buyer would only be alerted to the existence of the 1954 restrictive covenants if they are mentioned in the 1985 conveyance.

Disadvantages of unregistered land

The following summarises the flaws of unregistered land:

- The epitome of title could contain forged documents.
- Investigating title is time consuming (and therefore expensive).
- The bundle of title deeds may be lost, stolen or destroyed.
- Old documents can be very hard to read, particularly when hand written.
- If the epitome of title reveals no third party rights, a buyer may unwittingly purchase land burdened by such rights (see **7.3** below).

7.3 Enforceability of third party rights

Chapter 1 focused on the creation of legal and equitable interests in land. The focus of this chapter is whether a legal or equitable interest ('third party right') would bind a buyer of the land.

Section 205 LPA 1925 defines a 'Purchaser' to include a lessee (tenant), mortgagee (lender) or other person who for valuable consideration acquires an interest (including a mortgage) in property. The expression 'purchaser' is therefore more widely defined than a person purchasing a legal estate (for example a freehold or lease). The term 'buyer' is a more modern version of purchaser.

When a buyer investigates title, they are trying to discover if the land is subject to any third party rights that may bind them. In unregistered land, this will depend upon whether:

- the interest is legal or equitable; and
- how such an interest is protected.

7.3.1 Legal estates and rights

In unregistered land, an estate or interest:

- which is capable of being legal (it appears in s 1(1) or (2) LPA 1925); and
- which has been created using the correct formalities

creates a legal estate or interest (see **Chapter 1**).

Legal estates and interests bind the world. This means that the legal estate or interest binds any buyer (whether they knew of the interest or not).

The only exception to this rule is in relation to puisne mortgages which must be protected by a Land Charge. A puisne mortgage is a legal mortgage (or charge) which is not protected by the deposit of deeds. This will usually be a second mortgage, where the first mortgagee (lender) has already taken deposit of the deeds as part of its security.

Example 7.2

Alice has recently completed the purchase of Honeysuckle House consisting of a large house, self-contained annexe and a large garden ('the Property') from Belinda. Alice has discovered the following:

(a) Belinda created a right of way, by deed, in favour of the owner of the adjoining Rose Cottage.

(b) Tina has exclusive possession of the self-contained annexe for the following year and is paying market rent. Tina cannot produce any written evidence for this.

(c) Belinda created a mortgage, by deed, in favour of a Capital Bank Plc and deposited the title deeds to the Property with the bank.

Will Alice be bound by these interests?

Comment

Each interest is capable of being legal, being an easement, lease and mortgage respectively (see s 1(1) and (2) LPA 1925).

The easement and mortgage have been created by deed and therefore comply with the formalities required by s 52(1) LPA 1925 and s 1 LPMPA 1989. They are a legal easement and legal mortgage respectively.

The arrangement with Tina has the hallmarks of a lease as she has exclusive possession for a fixed duration. A lease is capable of being a legal estate (s 1(1)(b) LPA 1925). Usually, a lease must be created by deed in order to be legal (s 52(1) LPA 1925). However, the lease is for a duration of three years or less and meets the criteria in s 54(2) LPA 1925 (granted in possession, at the best rent reasonably obtainable and without a fine or premium) and, therefore, requires no formalities. It is a legal lease.

The easement, lease and mortgage are binding on Alice. They are legal estates or interests and therefore bind the world.

7.3.2 Equitable interests

Interests are equitable because either:

(a) the interest is not capable of being legal as it does not appear in s 1(1) or (2) LPA 1925; or

(b) the interest is capable of being legal but has not been created using the correct formalities.

Such interests are protected by either:

(a) a Land Charge; or

(b) the doctrine of notice.

7.3.3 Land Charges

Land Charges were introduced by the Land Charges Act (LCA) 1925 and came into force on 1 January 1926. They were intended as short-term method of protection for equitable interests (and puisne mortgages) with the assumption that all land in England and Wales would be registered very quickly. This has not happened, and the LCA 1925 has now been replaced by the LCA 1972.

Section 2 of the LCA 1972 sets out what can be protected by means of a Land Charge. If the interest does not appear in s 2 of the LCA 1972 then it cannot be protected as a Land Charge. The key classes for the purposes of this module are:

C(iv)	an estate contract
D(ii)	a restrictive covenant
D(iii)	an equitable easement
F	a home right
C(i)	puisne mortgage

How to register a Land Charge

A Land Charge is not registered against the parcel of land. Instead, it is registered against the estate owner in the version of their name as it appears in the deeds. This can cause difficulties:

- for holders of third-party rights with no access to the deeds; and
- where estate owners use different versions of their name.

The onus to register is on the person holding the equitable interest.

Example 7.3

Ashleigh enters into a contract for the creation of a lease in favour of Claire. This is an estate contract. In order to protect her estate contract, Claire would need to register a C(iv) Land Charge against Ashleigh's full name as it appears in the title deeds.

Effect of registering a Land Charge

Section 198 LPA 1925 confirms that registration of a Land Charge at the Land Charges Department (not Land Registry) is deemed to constitute actual notice of the interest as from the date of registration. Any buyer will, therefore, be bound by the interest (whether or not they know about it).

Effect of failure to register a Land Charge

In simple terms, a Land Charge is void against a buyer for money or money's worth of a legal estate unless the Land Charge is registered before completion of the purchase (s 4(6) LCA 1972).

Example 7.4

Continuing with Example 7.3: Ashleigh enters into a contract for the creation of a lease in favour of Claire. This is an estate contract. Claire fails to register a C(iv) Land Charge against Ashleigh's name. Ashleigh subsequently sells the land to Natasha for full market price.

Is Natasha bound by the estate contract?

Comment

Natasha is not bound. She has purchased a legal estate for money or money's worth and the Land Charge was not registered before completion of the purchase. Natasha takes free of the estate contract.

What if the buyer has actual knowledge of the interest?

A farmer granted his son an option to purchase the farm. An option is an estate contract. The son failed to register a C(iv) Land Charge. The farmer and son then fell out. The farmer subsequently conveyed the farm to his wife for the sum of £500 (much less than the true value of the farm). The son argued that his mother should be bound by his option as she knew about it when she purchased the land from her husband.

The court held that if a Land Charge was not protected by registration, the knowledge of the buyer is irrelevant. This was the outcome in *Midland Bank Trust Co Ltd v Green* [1981] 1 AC 513. The farmer's wife was not bound by her son's option.

Searching the Land Charges Register

The buyer of unregistered land will conduct a search of the Land Charges Register. Good practice is to search against all the names of estate owners revealed in the epitome of title, including any revealed who pre-date the root of title. This is because any Land Charge registered will bind the buyer.

Section 10 LCA 1972 provides that the search certificate from the Land Charges Register is conclusive in favour of the buyer (provided the buyer has searched the register as above).

Even if best practice is followed, it is possible that the buyer is bound by a Land Charge not revealed by the epitome of title. In these circumstances, the buyer may be entitled to statutory compensation where they suffer loss.

7.3.4 The doctrine of notice

The doctrine of notice is an equitable principle which has now been codified in s 199(1) LPA 1925. It applies to:

(a) equitable interests pre-dating 1925; and

(b) beneficial interests under a trust (express or implied) whenever created.

Equitable interests post-dating 1925 are protected by Land Charges. Beneficial interests under a trust cannot be protected by registration of a Land Charge. The doctrine of notice is their only means of protection.

A buyer is bound by equitable interests unless they are 'Equity's Darling'. This is a bona fide purchaser for value of a legal estate or interest without notice of the equitable interest. To break this down:

Bona fide

This means good faith. The buyer must act honestly and without fraudulent intent.

Purchaser for value

Consideration must be given for the purchase. Someone who has been gifted land is not a purchaser for value.

Value simply means some form of consideration. This could be nominal, for example £1.

Of the legal estate or interest

The buyer must be acquiring either a legal estate or a legal interest. The interest must appear in s 1(1) or (2) LPA 1925 and have met the formalities for the creation of a legal estate or interest. For example, buying the freehold (by deed) or taking a mortgage (by deed).

The buyer of an equitable interest cannot claim the benefit of the doctrine of notice and may therefore be bound by the third party right. This depends on which equitable right was created first. This is as a consequence of the equitable maxim: where the equities are equal the first in time will prevail.

Example 7.5

Joanne is the freehold owner of 4 Cherry Tree Close ('the Property'). Last year she granted a lease of the Property, by deed, for a term of five years to David. Last week, Joanne granted an option in favour of Sorcha for a period of one year to purchase the Property at an agreed price. Sorcha has checked the lease granted to David and discovered that Joanne's signature was not witnessed.

Is Sorcha bound by David's lease?

The lease to David is equitable as the document does not comply with the formalities for a deed (s 1 LPMPA 1989). However, equity would recognise the contract (*Parker v Taswell*).

Sorcha has an option. This is an equitable interest being an estate contract. At this stage, Sorcha has not acquired a legal estate or interest.

There are two equities: David's equitable lease and Sorcha's estate contract. The first in time will prevail. Sorcha will, therefore, be bound by David's equitable lease.

Without notice of the equitable interest

Does the buyer have notice of the third party's equitable interest? If so, the buyer will be bound. The onus is, therefore, on the buyer to prove that they have no form of notice. Notice comes in three forms:

- actual;
- constructive; and
- imputed.

Actual notice	The buyer must know of the existence of the equitable interest. For example, the seller may have alerted the buyer to its existence. Knowledge does not equate to rumour or gossip.
Constructive notice	The buyer is obliged to inspect the land, investigate the seller's title and make those enquiries which a reasonable person, with competent legal advice, would make. When inspecting the land, the buyer should be looking for indications of third-party rights. For example, a worn track indicating a right of way. The buyer should also be checking to see if anyone other than the seller is in occupation of the land. For example, as a result of a lease or a beneficial interest under a trust. When inspecting the land, the buyer is not obliged to look in the drawers or cupboards. If the buyer fails to make enquiries that a prudent buyer would, the buyer will have constructive notice of equitable interests.
Imputed notice	Most buyers appoint agents to assist them in the process of purchasing land. For example, a surveyor and/or a solicitor. If the buyer's agent has actual or constructive notice of an equitable interest, this will be imputed to the buyer. This is on the basis that the knowledge of the agent is assumed to be the knowledge of the principal (buyer).

If the buyer can demonstrate that they are a bona fide purchaser for value of the legal estate or interest without notice ('Equity's Darling'), they will take free of pre-1925 equitable interests and beneficial interests under a trust.

Example 7.6

Connor is the freehold owner of 56 Copeland Way ('the Property'). He has agreed to sell the Property to Fatima at a price of £235,000. Following exchange of contracts, Fatima discovers that Connor's wife, Lucy, has made significant contributions to the improvement of the property and claims a beneficial interest under a trust. When she inspected the Property, Fatima met Lucy but did not ask her if she claimed an interest in the Property.

Will Fatima be bound by Lucy's interest?

Comment

Fatima needs to demonstrate that she is a bona fide purchaser for value of the legal estate or interest without notice ('Equity's Darling'). There is no reason to doubt that Fatima is bona fide. She is a purchaser for value (£235,000) of the legal estate (the freehold). Fatima cannot prove that she is without notice. Fatima met Lucy but failed to make those enquiries which a reasonable person, with competent legal advice, would make. Fatima, therefore, has constructive notice of Lucy's beneficial interest under a trust. Fatima will be bound by Lucy's interest.

7.3.5 Overreaching

Overreaching is a mechanism by which a buyer can take property free of the interests of any person with a beneficial interest under a trust.

In order for overreaching to work, on completion the buyer must pay the purchase money (capital monies) to a minimum of two trustees (ss 2(1) and 27(2) LPA 1925). The trustees are the people who hold the legal estate. The interests of any person holding a beneficial interest under the trust then lift from the property and shift to the proceeds of sale (the purchase money).

Once overreaching has taken place, any beneficiary under a trust no longer has an interest in the property. Their interest is in the proceeds of sale. The buyer takes the property free of them.

Overreaching is only effective for beneficial interests under a trust.

Example 7.7

Returning to Example 7.6: the Property is in Connor's sole name and therefore there is only one trustee.

Fatima can take free of Lucy's interest if, prior to completion, Connor appoints a second trustee. Fatima would then pay the purchase money to a minimum of two trustees (Connor plus the second trustee) and Lucy's beneficial interest under a trust would lift from the Property and shift to the proceeds of sale. Fatima would then not be bound by Lucy's beneficial interest under a trust.

7.4 Approach

This builds on the approach outlined in **Chapter 1** (see **1.11**).

Take a step-by-step approach to unpacking a fact pattern to reach an answer. Do not assume that the existence of a deed means that a legal interest has been created. Always start with a basic analysis of the interest.

Once you have identified the nature of the interest, you can then analyse how and if it has been protected in unregistered land. This will enable you to determine whether or not the interest is binding on a buyer:

Step 1 – identify the interest

What hints do the facts provide as to the type of interest involved? The following may be helpful:

- Exclusive use for a fixed period = a lease.
- The right to use another landowner's land (but not creating exclusive possession) = an easement.
- An obligation not to do something on the land = a restrictive covenant.

Step 2 – is the interest capable of being legal, or is it equitable by nature?

Estates and interests which are capable of being legal appear in s 1(1) and (2) LPA 1925. If the interest does not appear in either sub-section then it is not capable of being legal. It is equitable by nature (s 1(3) LPA 1925).

Remember that an easement or profit must be created either forever or for a fixed duration to be capable of being legal (s 1(2)(a) LPA 1925).

Step 3 – have the correct formalities been used?

If the interest is capable of being legal, then a deed is required (s 52(1) LPA 1925), unless an exception applies. Check the facts carefully to ensure that a deed has been created (s 1 LPMPA 1989). If so, this creates a legal estate or interest.

Consider whether an exception may apply. Is the interest a short-term lease, ie possibly a parol lease?

If the interest is equitable by nature, the relevant formalities must be complied with unless the interest is an implied trust.

Step 4 – the interest is capable of being legal, but there is no deed

Equity may intervene to recognise the interest if there is:

- a contract;
- complying with s 2 LPMPA 1989; and
- capable of being specifically performed (he who seeks equity must do so with clean hands).

Step 5 – legal equitable or statutory?

By following steps 1 to 4 you can identify whether the interest is capable of being legal and whether it has been created validly. If the interest is equitable by nature (ie it is not capable of being legal) have the formalities for creation been followed?

Home rights do not create an interest in land and require no formalities for creation. They are statutory.

If the interest is capable of being legal but the formality rules have not been complied with *and* equity would not intervene, there would be no valid interest in land. The person claiming the right would have a licence only.

Step 6 – how should the right be protected in unregistered land?

If the interest is legal then it will be binding, binds the world.

If the interest is equitable:

- Can it be protected by a Land Charge?
- Is it a beneficial interest under a trust protected by the doctrine of notice?

Step 7 – has the interest been protected?

Has a Land Charge been registered? What is the consequence of failure to register?

If it is a beneficial interest under a trust:

- Does the buyer have notice?
- Has overreaching happened (did the buyer pay their purchase money to a minimum of two trustees)?

Step 8 – reach a conclusion

Example 7.8

Michael recently completed the purchase of an unregistered freehold property called Bluebell House ('the Property') from Tanya. The Property is a large house with two outbuildings (one large and one smaller outbuilding) and a large garden. Michael moved into the Property a few days ago and has since discovered the following issues:

(a) The larger outbuilding is occupied by Paul who uses it to store stock for his online retail business. Paul produced a document confirming that he has exclusive possession for 10 years from last year. Michael has checked the document and noted that Tanya's signature was not witnessed.

(b) The neighbouring landowner, Emily, has been to see Michael and produced a deed in which Tanya had promised not to use the Property for any trade or business. Michael recalls seeing a D(ii) Land Charge against Tanya's name before he completed the purchase of the Property.

(c) Tanya's husband, Christopher, has returned from a short holiday and asked Michael for his share of the sale proceeds. It transpired that Christopher had made significant improvements to the Property after he married Tanya.

Michael recalls meeting Christopher when he inspected the Property prior to exchange of contracts. Michael did not ask Christopher if he had any interest in the Property; and

(d) The small outbuilding is occupied by Kelly who uses the outbuilding to store her vintage clothes as part of her business. Kelly was unable to produce any document. Kelly states that Tanya allowed her exclusive possession of the outbuilding for a period of two years from last year. Kelly immediately took possession and has paid market rent ever since.

Will Michael be bound by the interests claimed by Paul, Emily, Christopher and Kelly?

Comment

Paul

The document grants Paul exclusive possession for a fixed duration. This indicates that a lease has been granted.

A lease is capable of being legal (s 1(1)(b) LPA 1925).

A deed is required to create a legal lease (s 52(1) LPA 1925). The document does not comply with the requirements of s 1 LPMPA 1989 as the landlord's signature has not been witnessed. It is, therefore, not a legal lease.

Equity may intervene and recognise an equitable lease if there is a:

- contract;
- complying with s 2 LPMPA 1989; and
- the contract is capable of being specifically performed.

An equitable lease is protected by registration of a C(iv) Land Charge. If a Land Charge has been registered then the equitable lease binds Michael. If not, an unregistered Land Charge is void against a purchaser of the legal estate for money or money's worth (s 4(6) LCA 1972). So, the equitable lease would not bind Michael.

Emily

A promise not to use the Property for any trade or business is a restrictive covenant.

A restrictive covenant does not appear in either s 1(1) or (2) LPA 1925 and is, therefore, equitable by nature (s 1(3) LPA 1925).

The relevant formality for the creation of a restrictive covenant is that it should be in writing and signed (s 53(1) LPA 1925). Here the restrictive covenant has been made by deed.

A restrictive covenant is protected in unregistered land by the registration of a D(ii) Land Charge. Michael recalls seeing such a registration against Tanya's name prior to his purchase of the Property. Michael is therefore bound by the restrictive covenant.

Christopher

Christopher has *two* possible interests in the Property:

- a beneficial interest under a trust; and
- home rights.

Each interest must be dealt with separately:

Beneficial interest under a trust

Christopher made significant improvements to the Property owned by Tanya. This is an implied trust.

An implied trust does not appear in either s 1(1) or (2) LPA 1925 and is therefore equitable by nature (s 1(3) LPA 1925).

There are no formalities for the creation of an implied trust (s 53(2) LPA 1925).

An implied trust is protected in unregistered land by the doctrine of notice (s 199 LPA 1925). Michael would need to demonstrate that he is a bona fide purchaser of the legal interest or estate for value without notice, ie 'Equity's Darling'.

Michael met Christopher when he inspected the Property but failed to ask Christopher any questions about his interest in the Property. Michael, therefore, has constructive notice of Christopher's beneficial interest under an implied trust.

Overreaching has not occurred as Michael paid his purchase money to only one trustee, Tanya. Michael is, therefore, bound by Christopher's beneficial interest under an implied trust.

Home rights

Christopher is also a non-owning spouse and, therefore, has home rights under s 30 FLA 1996.

There are no formalities for the creation of home rights.

Home rights are statutory rights and do not create an interest in land (s 30 FLA 1996).

Home rights are protected in unregistered land by the registration of a Class F Land Charge. If such a registration has been made, then Michael will be bound by the home rights. If not, Michael takes free.

Kelly

Kelly has exclusive possession for a fixed period. This is a lease.

A lease is capable of being legal (s 1(1)(b) LPA 1925).

Ordinarily, a lease would need to be made by deed to be legal. However, there are some exceptions, eg the parol lease.

The lease is for only two years and therefore may meet the criteria of section 54(2) LPA 1925 and require no formalities. Here, Kelly took immediate possession, is paying market rent and there is no fine or premium. A legal lease has been created.

In unregistered land, a legal lease binds the world. Michael is, therefore, bound by Kelly's lease.

Summary

- A seller of unregistered land must prove title by showing uninterrupted possession for a period of 15 years.
- A buyer of unregistered land must investigate title and inspect the land.
- Legal estates and rights (apart from puisne mortgages) bind the world meaning that a buyer will be bound by them whether or not the buyer knows about the estate or interest.
- Equitable interests (apart from a beneficial interest under a trust) are protected by registration of a Land Charge. Once registered the Land Charge is deemed to be actual notice and will, therefore, bind a buyer.
- An unregistered Land Charge is void against a purchaser of the legal estate for money or money's worth.
- A beneficial interest under a trust (express or implied) is protected by the doctrine of notice. The buyer takes free if they are a bona fide purchaser for value of the legal estate or interest with no notice ('Equity's Darling'). Notice can be actual, constructive or imputed.
- Beneficial interests under a trust can be overreached if the buyer pays their purchase money to a minimum of two trustees. The beneficial interests then lift from the land and attach to the proceeds of sale. The buyer takes free of such interests.

Sample questions

Question 1

A solicitor is acting for the seller of a freehold unregistered property. The solicitor is preparing for deduction of title to the property to the buyer's solicitor. They examine the deeds and documents relating to the property.

Which of the following is the best candidate for a good root of title when deducing title to the property?

A An assent of the property, dated 3 March 1983.

B A Land Charges certificate, dated 1 March 1983.

C A gift of the property, dated 10 June 1984.

D A conveyance of the property, dated 13 April 1985.

E A planning permission for the property, dated 5 August 2017.

Answer

The correct option is D. The conveyance would show the legal and equitable interests, is likely to contain a recognisable description and is unlikely to cast doubt on the title. Prior to the date of the conveyance in 1985, the purchaser's solicitor will have investigated title for the previous 15 years giving assurance to the buyer.

Title will not have been investigated in relation to the gift or the assent and therefore the conveyance is to be preferred over the assent. Options A and C are, therefore, incorrect.

Neither the Land Charges certificate nor the planning permission deal with the legal or equitable title to the property and are, therefore, not good roots of title. Options B and E are, therefore, wrong.

Question 2

A buyer recently completed the purchase of an unregistered freehold property ('the Property'). Yesterday, the buyer moved into the Property and was confronted by the neighbouring landowner who claimed to have a right of way over the Property for 20 years. The neighbouring landowner produced a deed evidencing the right of way. The buyer checked the document and discovered that the signatures had not been witnessed.

Will the buyer be bound by the neighbouring landowner's right of way?

A Yes, because the right of way is a legal right and, therefore, binding on the buyer.

B No, because the right of way is equitable by nature and, therefore, not binding on the buyer.

C No, because the right of way is legal but only binding if a Land Charge is registered.

D Yes, because the right of way is equitable and the buyer is bound by the equitable doctrine of notice.

E No, because the right of way is equitable and the buyer will only be bound if a Land Charge has been registered.

Answer

The correct option is E.

An easement for a fixed duration (20 years) is capable of being legal. A deed is required to create a legal easement. The document does not comply with the formalities for creating a deed because the signatures have not been witnessed. The easement is, therefore, equitable and would need to be protected by registration of a Land Charge.

Option A correctly states the legal principle but does not relate to the facts. The answer is, therefore, wrong.

Option B is partially correct in that it identifies that the easement is equitable but wrong in stating that an equitable easement cannot bind the buyer.

Option C is wrong as a legal easement in unregistered land would bind the world. A Land Charge is only required to protect an equitable easement.

Option D correctly states the legal principle applying to equitable easements created prior to 1926 but the easement in question was created recently and, therefore, the answer is wrong.

Question 3

A buyer purchases a freehold unregistered property ('the Property') from a husband and wife. Following completion of the purchase, the buyer is confronted by the wife's mother who claims that she has an interest in the Property. When the husband and wife originally bought the Property, the mother paid the deposit and has lived in the Property since the husband and wife bought it. The buyer recalls meeting the mother when inspecting the Property, but had no idea she had an interest in the Property.

Which of the following best describes whether the buyer will be bound by the mother's interest?

A The buyer will be bound as they have actual notice of the mother's interest.

B The buyer will not be bound as payment of the deposit is insufficient to create an interest in land.

C The buyer will be bound as they have constructive notice of the mother's interest.

D The buyer will not be bound as they have overreached the mother's interest.

E The buyer will be bound as the mother holds a legal interest which binds the world.

Answer

The correct option is D.

The mother made a direct financial contribution to the purchase price (the deposit) and this is unlikely to have been a gift. The mother holds a beneficial interest under a resulting trust. This is an equitable interest. Options B and E are, therefore, wrong.

The facts do not indicate that the buyer had actual knowledge of the mother's interest and option A is, therefore, wrong.

The buyer was likely to have constructive notice of the mother's interest on the basis that the buyer saw the mother when inspecting the property. This should have prompted the buyer to ask questions of the mother. However, the buyer paid the purchase monies to two trustees (the husband and wife) and this would overreach the mother's equitable interest. Option C is, therefore, not the best answer.

8 Registered Land

SQE1 syllabus

Registration of title to land:

- Estates that can be substantively registered
- How to protect interests
- Interests that override registration and interests that need to be protected on the register.

Note that for SQE1, candidates are not usually required to recall specific case names or cite statutory or regulatory authorities. Cases are provided for illustrative purposes only.

Learning outcomes

By the end of this chapter you will be able to apply relevant core legal principles and rules appropriately and effectively, at the level of a competent newly qualified solicitor in practice, to realistic client-based and ethical problems and situations in the following areas:

- Understand the form of a registered title
- Explain what must be registered
- Identify how third-party rights are protected in registered land
- Identify when an interest that overrides is relevant.

8.1 Proof of ownership

Land registration was introduced by the Land Registration Act (LRA) 1925 with the intention that all land in England and Wales would be registered. The process of registration has been slow and the 1925 legislation has now been replaced by the Land Registration Act (LRA) 2002, together with the Land Registration Rules. This was implemented on 13 October 2003.

Registered land is administered by Land Registry who maintain an electronic register. The register is openly accessible and, for a fee, anyone can obtain a copy of a register ('official copy').

The key aims of the LRA 2002 are:

- to extend the scope of first registration, so that more titles are registered; and
- that the register is a more complete reflection of the title ('the mirror principle').

The accuracy of the register is guaranteed by the State ('the insurance principle'). Any errors will usually be rectified and any person affected by rectification may claim compensation ('the indemnity principle').

8.2 The register

The form of register is electronic. Each title has its own unique title number. The register is divided into three parts:

- property register;
- proprietorship register; and
- charges register.

8.2.1 Property register

This contains a verbal description of the land and a reference to the title plan. The title plan shows edged in red the extent of the land which Land Registry (ie the State) guarantees.

It indicates the type of estate, freehold or leasehold.

Rights for the benefit of the registered title are set out in the property register.

8.2.2 Proprietorship register

This states the class of title. Absolute title is the best and most common grade. The Land Registry can award lesser grades of title, being possessory and qualified.

It gives the name and address of the registered proprietor.

It indicates any restrictions affecting the ability of the registered proprietor to deal with the legal estate in land.

8.2.3 Charges register

This contains notices of any registered third-party rights which burden the registered title (for example covenants, easements and mortgages). There will also be a note of any registrable leases created out of the estate.

Example 8.1

Candice is the owner of 13 Goodwin Avenue ('the Property'). The Property is registered freehold land. Candice purchased the Property with the assistance of a mortgage from Friendly Bank Plc.

Candice has a right of way over a shared drive part of which is on her neighbour's land. The Property is subject to a restrictive covenant that Candice cannot use the Property for any trade or business.

Where would you find these interests in the registered title?

Comment

The mortgage	In the charges register. There will be two entries. The first will identify the registered charge and the date it was created. The second entry identifies the proprietor of the charge, Friendly Bank Plc.
Easement	In the property register as the right of way benefits the Property.
Restrictive covenant	In the charges register as the restrictive covenant is a burden on the land.

8.3 First registration

First registration is the process by which the title deeds and documents in unregistered title are translated to a registered title. Once registered, the title deeds and documents have no further purpose and, subsequently, the registered title is deduced by official copies extracted by Land Registry.

Section 4(1) LRA 2002 sets out the trigger events for first registration. The list of events triggering first registration is wider than the original LRA 1925 with the purpose of ensuring that more land in England and Wales is registered.

The events which are subject to compulsory first registration are set out in **8.3.1** below.

8.3.1 Qualifying estates

A qualifying estate is defined as:

- unregistered freehold estate; and
- unregistered leasehold estate with more than seven years to run.

The transfer of a qualifying estate by sale, gift, court order or assent triggers first registration.

An assent is where personal representatives transfer land to a beneficiary under a will.
An example of a court order would be on divorce, where one party to the marriage transfers the matrimonial home to the other in compliance of a court order.

Example 8.2

Yang acquires the titles below. Which events trigger an application for first registration?

Estate	**Must be registered**	**Not subject to first registration**
The sale of an unregistered lease with 75 years to run		
A freehold unregistered property gifted by his father		

(continued)

(*continued*)

Estate	Must be registered	Not subject to first registration
The sale of an unregistered lease with five years left to run		
The sale of an unregistered lease with 50 years to run pursuant to a court order		
The sale of an unregistered freehold estate		

Comment

The only estate that is not subject to compulsory first registration is the transfer of an unregistered lease with five years left to run. All the other estates are included within the definition of a qualifying estate and would trigger an application for first registration.

Procedure

The buyer of an unregistered estate follows the process outlined in **Chapter 1**:

- investigates the unregistered title;
- inspects the land; and
- searches the Land Charges Register (as the land is currently unregistered land).

In addition, the buyer checks the register of cautions against first registration held by Land Registry. A caution against first registration can be registered by a person who claims an interest in unregistered land. It has no substantive effect, but alerts the cautioner to an application for first registration.

Voluntary registration

Qualifying estate owners can apply for voluntary registration at any time (s 3 LRA 2002). There is a fee discount for such an application as an incentive for land owners to register.

8.3.2 Legal leases

A legal lease created (granted) for more than seven years must be registered. On registration, the lease will be given its own title number. This means that one parcel of land may have more than one registered title, a freehold registered title and a leasehold registered title.

The registration of a legal lease for more than seven years does not trigger the registration of the freehold reversion. It is possible to have an unregistered freehold title with a registered lease.

Legal leases for seven years or less are protected as overriding interests. **See 8.8.1**.

8.3.3 Mortgages

The creation of a first legal mortgage of a qualifying estate triggers first registration of the estate mortgaged. Thus, a mortgage of freehold unregistered land or the mortgage of an unregistered lease with more than seven years to run would trigger the registration of the freehold or lease respectively.

8.3.4 Time limits for first registration

The buyer must apply for first registration within two months of the triggering event, the transfer, grant of the lease, gift or assent (s 6 LRA 2002). If this time limit is not observed, the effect is that:

(a) in the case of a transfer, the legal estate reverts to the transferor. An equitable interest is held until registration has been completed;

(b) in the case of the grant of a legal lease, the transaction fails to grant a legal lease. An equitable interest is held until registration has been completed; and

(c) in the case of the creation of a mortgage, the transaction fails to create a legal mortgage. An equitable mortgage exists until registration has been completed.

The Land Registry may extend the period for registration if there is a good reason.

8.4 Registrable dispositions

Title is already registered ('a registered estate'). This could be a freehold or a lease for more than seven years.

Once registered, certain transactions ('registrable dispositions') will only have legal effect if they too are registered (s 27 LRA 2002). These include:

(a) the transfer of a registered estate;

(b) the grant of a legal lease for more than seven years out of a registered estate. On registration, this will be given its own title number and title register. It will also appear in the charges register of the landlord's title within the schedule of leases, as it burdens the landlord's title;

(c) the grant of a legal charge. This will appear in the charges register of the borrower's title (s 27(2)(f) LRA 2002). A registered charge is shown by two entries. The first identifies that there is a charge and the date of creation. The second identifies the proprietor of the charge (the lender); and

(d) an expressly granted legal easement or profit (s 27(2)(d) LRA 2002). This must be registered against the title to which it relates. It will also appear in the charges register of the servient land.

8.5 Priority of mortgages

A mortgage over a registered title is a registrable disposition under s 27(2)(f) LRA 2002. It will become a legal mortgage only when it is entered in the charges register of the title affected.

Where there is more than one charge registered against the title, the order for priority depends on the order in which they are entered on the register (s 48 LRA 2002) and not the date of creation of the charges. This means that the mortgage that appears first in time will rank first (ie be paid first from the proceeds of sale). (See **Chapters 5** and **9**.)

8.6 Interests affecting a registered estate

Interests affecting a registered estate (IAREs) are third party interests in land which are not:

- capable of substantive registration (an estate in land);
- set out in s 27 LRA 2002 as registrable dispositions; or
- overriding interests.

We will see later in this chapter that there is an interrelationship between IAREs and overriding interests.

IAREs include (but are not limited to):

- estate contracts;
- home rights;
- interests under a trust;
- equitable easements or profits created after 2003;
- equitable leases; and
- restrictive covenants.

By s 29(1) LRA 2002, a purchaser of a registered title for valuable consideration takes free of unprotected IAREs. Such interests are protected by means of either a notice or a restriction.

8.6.1 Restrictions

Interests under a trust of land (whether express or implied) are protected by a restriction (s 40 LRA 2002). The restriction appears in the proprietorship register. It alerts a buyer that the registered proprietor has a limited right to deal with the legal estate in the land and that the buyer needs to implement overreaching in order to take free of the trust interest. See **8.7**.

Entry of a restriction will prevent the registration of a later registrable disposition for value which is not in accordance with the terms of the restriction.

A restriction may be entered onto the register without the consent of the registered proprietor.

8.6.2 Notices

Notices apply to other interests (other than interests under a trust of land). A notice appears in the charges register (s 32 LRA 2002).

A notice may be entered onto the register without the consent of the registered proprietor.

A trust of land cannot be protected by registration of a notice (s 33 LRA 2002).

The registered proprietor can challenge a notice and claim damages for any loss suffered.

8.7 Overreaching

Overreaching is a mechanism by which a buyer can take property free of the interests of any person with a beneficial interest under a trust.

In order for overreaching to work, on completion the buyer must pay the purchase money (capital monies) to a minimum of two trustees (ss 2(1) and 27(2) LPA 1925). The trustees are the people who hold the legal estate. The interests of any person holding a beneficial interest under the trust then lift from the property and shift to the proceeds of sale (the purchase money).

Once overreaching has taken place, any beneficiary under a trust no longer has an interest in the property. Their interest is in the proceeds of sale. The buyer takes the property free of the trust interest.

Overreaching is only effective for beneficial interests under a trust. It *cannot* be used in respect of any other third party interest.

Example 8.3

Tom and Sally purchase Bleak House ('the Property') with the help of Sally's parents, Gary and Amy. Tom and Sally are the freehold registered proprietors of the Property. Gary and Amy contributed half the purchase price and occupy the Property.

A year later, Tom and Sally's business is struggling financially and they obtain a loan in return for the grant of a mortgage over the Property in favour of City of London Building Society ('the Lender'). Tom and Sally default on the loan and the Lender seeks to exercise its power of sale to recover the money it is owed.

Is the Lender bound by Gary and Amy's interest?

Comment

Gary and Amy hold a beneficial interest under a resulting trust. The Lender is not bound by their interest because the purchase monies (here the loan advance) was paid to two trustees (Tom and Sally). Overreaching has occurred and Gary and Amy's interest has lifted from the Property and shifted to the proceeds of sale.

8.8 Interests which override

Overriding interests were introduced by the LRA 1925. These are interests that do not appear on the register but bind the owner of the legal estate and any buyer of it. In the LRA 1925 overriding interests were:

- legal easements;
- leases not exceeding 21 years; and
- rights of persons in actual occupation.

The LRA 2002 reduced the scope of overriding interests in order to make the register a better reflection of reality. The LRA 2002 is less broad and less generous than the LRA 1925 in this respect. However, the case law relating to the LRA 1925 remains useful in understanding overriding interests.

In accordance with s 29 LRA 2002, a buyer for valuable consideration of registered land takes free of all interests save for:

- registered charges;
- those registered as a notice in the register; and
- interests which override in Schedule 3.

Schedule 3 LRA 2002 contains three paragraphs as follows:

8.8.1 Paragraph 1

> A leasehold estate in land granted for a term not exceeding seven years from the date of the grant.

The word 'granted' means that the lease is a legal lease. Remember that legal leases for three years or less can be created informally (ie not created by deed), provided they meet the criteria of s 54(2) LPA 1925 (ie parol leases).

Paragraph 1 applies to fixed term and periodic leases (provided the period does not exceed seven years).

Legal leases for more than seven years must be registered as they are registrable dispositions (s 27 LRA 2002). Legal leases for seven years or less are automatically protected by paragraph 1, including parol leases.

Example 8.4

Georgina is the freehold registered proprietor of 77 Sandy Lane ('the Property'). Last year, Georgina granted a lease, by deed, for a period of five years to Harry. Georgina has now sold the Property to Ola.

Is Ola bound by the lease to Harry?

Comment

Yes. The lease is a legal lease (created by deed) and the period does not exceed seven years. It is, therefore, not a registrable disposition, and so, cannot be registered. However, it is automatically protected as an interest that overrides under Sch 3, para 1 LRA 2002.

8.8.2 Paragraph 3

This protects legal easements and profits created by implication or prescription after 12 October 2003. Such easements/profits do not require a deed in order to be legal and can be implied by:

- necessity
- common intention
- *Wheeldon v Burrows*
- s 62 LPA 1925

or created by prescription.

See **Chapter 3** for how these easements are created.

They will take effect as overriding interests if one of the three conditions is satisfied in Sch 3, para 3 LRA 2002:

(i) the purchaser has actual knowledge of the easement or profit on the date of the transfer in their favour; *or*

(ii) the existence of the right would have been apparent on a reasonably careful inspection of the land over which the easement or profit is exercisable; *or*

(iii) if the easement or profit has been exercised least once in the year prior to the land transfer.

Example 8.5

Marcel recently purchased the freehold registered title to 52 Lark Rise ('the Property') and upon moving in has discovered that Agnes, who lives at 54 Lark Rise, has been using a shortcut every Tuesday across the Property to reach the village hall for her Women's Institute meeting since 1998.

Is Marcel bound by Agnes' shortcut?

Comment

The facts state Agnes lives at 54 Lark Rise, but not whether she is the freehold owner. If she is a tenant, then she cannot acquire prescriptive rights.

Assuming that Agnes is the freehold owner, she has exercised the right continuously (once a week) and as of right (nothing in the facts to suggest otherwise) for over 20 years creating an easement by prescription.

Such an easement is protected as an overriding interest under Sch 3, para 3 LRA 2002 provided one of the criteria is met. Here, the right has been used at least once in the year preceding the disposition to Marcel. This means that Marcel is bound by the easement.

8.9 Schedule 3, para 2 LRA 2002

An interest belonging at the time of the disposition to a person in actual occupation, so far as relating to land of which they are in actual occupation.

Paragraph 2 creates a safety net for unprotected IAREs but only if the person with the interest is in 'actual occupation'. Paragraph 2 only works if there is:

An interest (proprietary) + Actual occupation

Example 8.6

Amelia had an equitable lease of a flat in London. She has not protected this by registration of a notice. She keeps some furniture and clothes at the flat but does not live there. Her stepson lives in the flat with her permission (as he was separated from his wife). He occupies the flat as a licensee, an arrangement that gives him no proprietary rights in land.

Amelia's landlord sold the freehold reversion and the buyer wants to repossess the flat. Amelia argues that she had an overriding interest or that her stepson does.

Would the buyer be bound by Amelia's interest?

Comment

No. Neither Amelia nor her stepson hold an overriding interest on the basis that:

- Amelia has an interest in land, but no actual occupation; and
- the stepson has actual occupation, but no interest in land.

Therefore, neither satisfy the requirement in Sch 3, para 2 for an interest, plus actual occupation.

8.9.1 What is an interest?

Generally, every type of property right in land can be an overriding interest provided it satisfies the requirements of Sch 3, para 2 (eg a beneficial interest under the trust of land, and equitable lease or option).

However, there are specific exceptions, as follows:

(a) personal rights cannot be upgraded to overriding status as they do not create a property right in land (eg contractual licences);

(b) home rights are excluded by s 31(10)(b) FLA 1996. A statutory right of occupation cannot be overriding despite the person being in actual occupation; and

(c) easements as the exercise of an easement is mere user of the land and cannot amount to actual occupation.

8.9.2 What does occupation mean?

There is no statutory definition of 'actual occupation'. There are a number of cases which are helpful both from the LRA 1925 and the LRA 2002.

In *Williams and Glyn's Bank v Boland* [1981] AC 487 the court stated that:

(a) the words ***actual occupation*** are ordinary words of plain English and should be interpreted as such;

(b) the word ***actual*** emphasises that physical presence is required; and

(c) ***occupation*** is a question of fact.

The concept of occupation was further developed in *Abbey National Building Society v Cann* [1991] 1 AC 56 with the following principles:

(a) ***occupation*** is a concept which may have different connotations according to the nature and purpose of the property which is claimed to be occupied;

(b) it does not necessarily involve the ***personal presence*** of the person claiming the interest in land. A caretaker or a representative of a company can occupy; and

(c) occupation does involve some *degree of* ***permanence and continuity*** which would rule out mere fleeting presence.

8.9.3 Temporary absence (residential property)

What is the effect of the occupier being temporarily absent? If there is:

- visible evidence of occupation, eg furniture and possessions; and
- an intention to return to the property

then the person remains in actual occupation.

In *Chhokar v Chhokar* [1984] Fam Law 269 the husband was the sole legal owner and secretly sold the house whilst his wife was in hospital (giving birth). The court found that the presence of her furniture in the house provided evidence of her continuing occupation and her intention to return. She was, therefore, in actual occupation, despite her temporary absence.

In *Link Lending v Bustard* [2010] EWCA Civ 424 the claimant was involuntarily detained in a psychiatric unit. Her possessions and furniture remained at the property to which she made weekly supervised visits. The court found that the relevant factors in determining whether somebody is in actual occupation include:

- the degree of permanence and continuity of presence;
- the intentions and wishes of that person;
- the length of absence and reason for it;
- the nature of the property; and
- the personal circumstances of the person.

The court found that the involuntary residence elsewhere together with a persistent intention to return home when possible was sufficient for the claimant to be in actual occupation.

8.9.4 Commercial property

Lord Oliver in *Abbey National Building Society v Cann* said:

> Occupation is a concept which may have different connotations according to the nature and purpose of the property.

In *Kling v Keston Properties Ltd* (1983) 49 P&CR 212 a car was parked regularly in a garage. It was held that this was the normal use of the garage and could amount to actual occupation.

In *Malory Enterprises v Cheshire Homes* [2002] Ch 216 the land in question was derelict with disused buildings and open land. The claimants were found to be in occupation on the basis that they had:

- erected fences;
- put up 'no trespassing' signs;
- replaced wooden fencing with high security steel fence to prevent vandalism; and
- replaced a lock that had been broken.

The key principles from the case are:

(a) what constitutes actual occupation of property depends on the nature and state of the property (affirming *Cann*); and

(b) there must be some physical presence with some degree of permanence and continuity to be sufficient to put someone inspecting the land on notice.

In *Thomas v Clydesdale Bank Plc* [2010] EWHC 2755 (QB), Ms Thomas claimed a beneficial interest under a constructive trust and an overriding interest under Sch 3, para 2 LRA 2002. The property was uninhabitable due to ongoing renovations. Ms Thomas visited the property every other day and there were builders and an interior designer on site. Ms Thomas had reasonable prospects of establishing:

- that there was a degree of permanence and continuity in her presence;
- that her intention and wish was to reside permanently at the property; and
- that her presence was sufficient for the nature of the property in the course of renovation.

8.9.5 Exceptions

Overriding status under Sch 3, para 2 will be lost if:

(a) the person holding the interest has failed to disclose the right, upon inquiry, when they could reasonably have been expected to do so. This envisages that there will be situations where it is not reasonable to expect someone to respond to an enquiry by revealing their right. It depends on the facts; and

(b) the person's occupation was not obvious on a reasonably careful inspection unless the buyer has actual knowledge.

Therefore, for a successful claim to an overriding interest a person needs either:

INTEREST (PROPRIETARY) + OBVIOUS ACTUAL OCCUPATION

OR

INTEREST (PROPRIETARY) + NON-OBVIOUS ACTUAL OCCUPATION + ACTUAL KNOWLEDGE

In *Thomas v Clydesdale Bank Plc* [2010] EWHC 2755 (QB) the court found that it is the visible signs of occupation which have to be *obvious on inspection*:

> ...in order to determine whether somebody is in actual occupation it is necessary to determine not only matters which would be obvious on inspection but matters which would require enquiry to ascertain them. That includes such things as the permanence and continuity of the presence of the person concerned, the intentions of wishes of that person and the personal circumstances of the person concerned.

Example 8.6

Benjamin is the sole registered freehold owner of 12 Hartington Road ('the Property'). Benjamin's wife, Harriet, has made significant contributions towards the payment of the mortgage. She has never sought to protect her interest. Whilst Harriet was away for two weeks taking care of her elderly mother, Benjamin sold the Property to Cameron. Benjamin concealed all of Harriet's possessions prior to Cameron inspecting the Property. Cameron has no knowledge of Harriet's interest.

Is Cameron bound by Harriet's interest?

Comment

No. Harriet has a beneficial interest under a constructive trust. She has not sought to protect her interest, and therefore, there would be no restriction in the proprietorship register. Harriet is in actual occupation as she has left her possessions in the Property and has a *settled intention* to return. However, Harriet loses overriding status on the basis that her occupation is not obvious on a reasonably careful inspection (due to Benjamin concealing her possessions). Cameron is not, therefore, bound by Harriet's interest and her only recourse lies against Benjamin.

8.10 Approach

This builds on the approach outlined in **Chapter 1** (see **1.11**).

Take a step-by-step approach to unpacking a fact pattern to reach an answer. Do not assume that the existence of a deed means that a legal interest has been created.

Always start with a basic analysis of the interest.

Once you have identified the nature of the interest you can then analyse how, and if, it has been protected in registered land. This will enable you to determine whether or not the interest is binding on a buyer.

Step 1 – identify the interest

What hints do the facts provide as to the type of interest involved? The following may be helpful:

- exclusive use for a fixed period = a lease
- the right to use another landowner's land (but not creating exclusive possession) = an easement
- an obligation not to do something on the land = a restrictive covenant

Step 2 – is the interest capable of being legal, or is it equitable by nature?

Estates and interests which are capable of being legal appear in ss 1(1) and (2) LPA 1925. If the interest does not appear in either sub-section, then it is not capable of being legal. It is equitable by nature (s 1(3) LPA 1925), unless it is a statutory right.

Remember that an easement or profit must be created either forever or for a fixed duration to be capable of being legal (s 1(2)(a) LPA 1925).

Step 3 – have the correct formalities being used?

If the interest is capable of being legal, then a deed is required (s 52(1) LPA 1925), unless an exception applies. Check the facts carefully to ensure that a deed has been created (s 1 LPMPA 1989). If so, this creates a legal estate or interest.

Consider whether an exception may apply. For example, is the interest a short-term lease?

If the interest is equitable by nature, the relevant formalities must be complied with unless the interest is an implied trust.

Step 4 – the interest is capable of being legal, but there is no deed

Equity may intervene to recognise the interest if there is:

- a contract;
- complying with s 2 LPMPA 1989; and
- capable of being specifically performed.

Step 5 – legal equitable or statutory?

By following steps 1 to 4 you can identify whether the interest is capable of being legal and whether it has been created validly. If the interest is equitable by nature (it is not capable of being legal), have the formalities for creation been followed?

Home rights under s 30 FLA 1996 do not create an interest in land and require no 'land' formalities for creation. There are, however, a number of conditions set out in the FLA 1996 which must be complied with if the home right is to be available to the spouse/civil partner.

If the interest is capable of being legal, but the formality rules have not been complied with *and* equity would not intervene, there would be no valid interest in land. The person claiming the right would have a licence only.

Step 6 – how should the right be protected in registered land?

Is it:

- a registrable estate?
- a registrable disposition?
- protected as an overriding interest in Sch 3, para 1 or 3?
- an IARE?
- upgraded to overriding status under Sch 3, para 2?

Step 7 – has the interest been protected?

What do the facts tell you?

If it is a beneficial interest under a trust (whether or not there is a restriction in the proprietorship register) has overreaching taken place (did the buyer pay their purchase money to a minimum of two trustees)?

Step 8 – reach a conclusion

Example 8.7

*The facts are very similar to those in **Example 7.8** in **Chapter 7.***

Michael recently completed the purchase of a registered freehold property called Bluebell House ('the Property') from Tanya. The Property is a large house with two outbuildings (one large and one smaller outbuilding) and a large garden. Michael moved into the Property a few days ago and has since discovered the following issues:

(a) *The larger outbuilding is occupied by Paul who uses it to store stock for his online retail business. Paul produced a document confirming that he has exclusive possession for 10 years from last year and that he paid a single premium as payment for the grant of the lease. Michael has checked the document and noted that Tanya's signature has not been witnessed.*

(b) *The neighbouring landowner, Emily, has been to see Michael and produced a deed in which Tanya had promised only to use the Property as a single private home with no trade or business. Michael recalls seeing something about this in the charges register of the title before he completed the purchase of the Property.*

(c) *Tanya's husband, Christopher, has returned from a short holiday and asked Michael for his share of the sale proceeds. It transpired that Christopher had made significant improvements to the Property after he married Tanya. Michael recalls seeing nothing in the title to reflect this. Michael recalls meeting Christopher when he inspected the Property prior to exchange of contracts. Michael did not ask Christopher if he had any interest in the Property.*

(d) *The small outbuilding is occupied by Kelly who uses the outbuilding to store her vintage clothes as part of her business. Kelly was unable to produce any document. Kelly states that Tanya allowed her exclusive possession of the outbuilding for a period of two years from last year. Kelly immediately took possession and has paid market rent ever since.*

Will Michael be bound by the interests claimed by Paul, Emily, Christopher and Kelly?

Comment

Paul

The document grants Paul exclusive possession for a fixed duration. This indicates that a lease has been granted.

A lease is capable of being legal (s 1(1)(b) LPA 1925).

A deed is required to create a legal lease (s 52(1) LPA 1925). The document does not comply with the requirements of s 1 LPMPA 1989 as the landlord's signature has not been witnessed. The parol lease exception does not apply as it is for a term in excess of three years and a single fine/premium was paid. It is, therefore, not a legal lease.

Equity may intervene and recognise an equitable lease if there is a:

- contract;
- complying with s 2 LPMPA 1989; and
- the contract is capable of being specifically performed.

An equitable lease is protected by registration of a notice in the charges register. There is no mention of this in the facts. Therefore, prima facie, it would appear that Michael will not be bound by the lease.

However, Paul may have an overriding interest under Sch 3, para 2, if he can show:

- he has an interest (proprietary) - an equitable lease is a proprietary interest;
- he is in actual occupation - storage of stock in an outbuilding may be sufficient to indicate permanence and continuity; and
- his occupation is obvious on a reasonably careful inspection - the presence of stock would amount to visible signs of occupation.

Paul's interest would be binding on Michael as an overriding interest under Sch 3, para 2, notwithstanding the fact Paul failed to properly protect the lease by registration of a notice in the charges register.

Emily

A promise to use the Property as a single private home is a restrictive covenant.

A restrictive covenant does not appear in either s 1(1) or (2) LPA 1925 and is, therefore, equitable by nature (s 1(3) LPA 1925).

The relevant formality for the creation of a restrictive covenant is in writing and signed (s 53(1) LPA 1925). Here the restrictive covenant has been made by deed, which more than complies with the relevant formality.

A restrictive covenant is protected in registered land by the registration of a notice in the charges register. Michael recalls seeing such a registration in the register prior to his purchase of the Property. Michael is, therefore, bound by the restrictive covenant.

Christopher

Christopher has two possible interests in the Property:

- a beneficial interest under a trust; and
- home rights.

Each interest must be dealt with separately:

Beneficial interest under a trust

Christopher made significant improvements to the Property owned by Tanya. This is an implied trust.

An implied trust does not appear in either s 1(1) or (2) LPA 1925 and is, therefore, equitable by nature (s 1(3) LPA 1925).

There are no formalities for the creation of an implied trust (s 53(2) LPA 1925).

A restriction does not appear to have been registered. Christopher may have an overriding interest under Sch 3, para 2 if he can show:

- he has an interest (proprietary) – a beneficial interest under an implied trust is a proprietary interest;
- he is in actual occupation – Christopher was temporarily absent but clearly intended to return and presumably left his possessions in the Property; and
- his occupation is obvious on a reasonably careful inspection – Michael met Christopher at the property and cannot rely on the exception as Michael did not ask Christopher about his interest.

Christopher's interest would be binding on Michael.

Overreaching has not occurred as Michael paid his purchase money to only one trustee, Tanya. Michael is, therefore, bound by Christopher's beneficial interest under an implied trust.

Home rights

Christopher is also a non-owning spouse and, therefore, has home rights under s 30 FLA 1996.

There are no 'land' formalities for the creation of home rights, although the FLA 1996 sets out a number of requirements.

Home rights are statutory rights and do not create an interest in land (s 30 FLA 1996).

Home rights are protected in registered land by the registration of a notice in the charges register. Michael did not see such an entry and, therefore, is not bound by Christopher's home rights.

Kelly

Kelly has exclusive possession for a fixed period. This is a lease.

A lease is capable of being legal (s 1(1)(b) LPA 1925).

The lease is for only two years and, therefore, may meet the criteria of s 54(2) LPA 1925 and require no formalities (parol lease). Here, Kelly took immediate possession, is paying market rent and there is no fine or premium. A legal lease has been created.

In registered land, a legal lease for seven years or less is automatically binding as an overriding interest in Sch 3, para 1 LRA 2002.

Summary

- In registered land title is proved by Official Copies of the register.
- The register is in three parts:
  - the property register (containing a description of the property and any rights benefiting the land);
  - the proprietorship register; and
  - the charges register (containing charges and other notices burdening the land).
- A buyer of registered land must investigate title and inspect the land.
- The sale, gift or assent of a qualifying estate and the creation of a mortgage triggers an application for first registration of unregistered land.

- In registered land, registrable dispositions (s 27 LRA 2002) must be completed by registration in order to be legal (s 29 LRA 2002).
- Equitable interests (and home rights) are protected as IAREs by entry of:
  - a restriction in the proprietorship register (in the case of a beneficial interest under a trust); and otherwise
  - a notice in the charges register (including home rights).
- Leases for seven years or less and certain types of easements and profits are automatically binding as overriding interests under Sch 3, para 1 and para 3 respectively.
- Unprotected interests can be upgraded to overriding status if they meet the criteria in Sch 3, para 2. This is, broadly, an interest (proprietary) in land, plus obvious actual occupation.
- Beneficial interests under a trust can be overreached if the buyer pays their purchase money to a minimum of two trustees. The beneficial interest then lifts from the land and attaches to the proceeds of sale. The buyer takes free of such interests.

Sample questions

Question 1

A solicitor is acting for the buyer of a freehold registered property ('the Property'). The seller tells the buyer that the Property is burdened by a restrictive covenant.

What will the buyer's solicitor look for when examining the official copies of the title to the Property to confirm that the restrictive covenant is properly registered?

A An entry referring to a restrictive covenant in the property register.

B A restriction on dealings in the proprietorship register.

C An entry referring to a restrictive covenant in the proprietorship register.

D An entry referring to a restrictive covenant in the charges register.

E An entry referring to an easement in the charges register.

Answer

The correct option is D. Interests that burden a registered title are found in the charges register.

Question 2

A buyer recently completed the purchase of a registered freehold property ('the Property'). Yesterday, the buyer moved into the Property and was confronted by the neighbouring landowner who claimed to have a lease of the Property for five years from last year and granted by deed.

Will the buyer be bound by the neighbour's lease?

A Yes, because the lease is a legal right and, therefore, binds the world.

B No, because the lease is equitable by nature and, therefore, not binding on the buyer.

C Yes, because it is a legal lease for a term of seven years or less, and so, automatically protected as an overriding interest.

D No, because the lease is a legal lease, and so, should have been registered substantively.

E No, because the lease is equitable and the buyer will only be bound if a notice has been registered.

Answer

The correct option is C.

A lease is capable of being legal. In order to be legal it must be created by deed (s 52(1) LPA 1925). The facts state that the lease is made by deed. Options B and E are, therefore, wrong.

The lease is for five years and, therefore, cannot be registered as a registrable disposition. Option D is, therefore, wrong.

A five-year legal lease is automatically protected as an overriding interest (Sch 3, para 1 LRA 2002). Option A is, therefore, wrong as it relates to unregistered land and the facts state that the Property is registered.

Question 3

A buyer purchases a freehold registered property ('the Property') from a seller. Following completion of the purchase, the buyer is confronted by the seller's wife who claims that she has an interest in the Property. After their marriage, the wife moved into the Property and paid half the mortgage payments. When the buyer checked the title, there was nothing to indicate that the wife had any interest in the Property. The buyer recalls meeting the wife when inspecting the Property and noted the wife's furniture and possessions, but did not ask the wife if she had any interest in the Property.

Which of the following best describes whether the buyer will be bound by the wife's interest?

A The buyer will be bound as they have actual notice of the wife's interest.

B The buyer will not be bound as payment of the mortgage is insufficient to create an interest in land.

C The buyer will not be bound as they have overreached the wife's interest.

D The buyer will be bound as the wife holds a legal interest which binds the world.

E The buyer will be bound as the wife has an overriding interest as she has obvious actual occupation.

Answer

The correct option is E.

The wife has a beneficial interest under a constructive trust as she made a direct financial contribution (paying the mortgage) and this conduct would be sufficient to infer a common intention to share the Property beneficially. Option B is, therefore, wrong.

A beneficial interest under a constructive trust is equitable and, therefore, option D is wrong.

The facts indicate that there was nothing on the register of title to indicate the wife's interest meaning that there was no restriction in the proprietorship register. The buyer, therefore, had no actual knowledge of the wife's interest and option A is wrong.

The buyer paid the purchase money to only one trustee and, therefore, has not overreached the wife's beneficial interest under a constructive trust. Option C is, therefore, wrong.

The wife has an overriding interest under Sch 3, para 2 as she has a proprietary interest (a beneficial interest under a constructive trust) and is in actual occupation (the facts state that the wife has occupied the Property since her marriage to the seller). The wife's occupation was obvious on a reasonable inspection as the buyer noted both her presence and that of her possessions at the Property. The overriding interest was capable of being overreached but, as stated above, the buyer paid the purchase money to only one trustee.

9 Consolidation

Learning outcomes

By the end of this chapter you will be able to apply relevant core legal principles and rules appropriately and effectively, at the level of a competent newly qualified solicitor in practice, to realistic client-based and ethical problems and situations in relation to third party rights in unregistered and registered land in the following areas:

- Co-ownership and trusts of land
- Easements
- Freehold covenants
- Mortgages
- Leases.

9.1 Introduction

The purpose of this chapter is to show how third party rights in unregistered and registered land (from **Chapters 7** and **8** respectively) are relevant to each topic of substantial land law from **Chapters 2** to **6**. Each section relates to an earlier chapter and includes examples to work through using the approach set out at **1.11** (and further developed in **Chapters 7** and **8**).

9.2 Co-ownership and trusts of land (Chapter 2) and home rights

When purchasing co-owned land, will the purchaser (widely defined to include a tenant and a mortgagee) be bound by the equitable interests held by any beneficiary?

A beneficial/equitable interest under a trust is equitable by nature – s 1(3) LPA 1925. The relevant formalities are:

- in the case of an express trust – in writing and signed (s 53(1) LPA 1925); and
- there are no formalities for the creation of an implied trust (resulting or constructive) – s 53(2) LPA 1925.

9.2.1 Overreaching

If overreaching has occurred, the buyer will take free of any beneficial interests under a trust.

In order for overreaching to work, on completion the buyer must pay the purchase money (capital monies) to a minimum of two trustees (ss 2(1) and 27(2) LPA 1925). The interests of any person holding a beneficial interest under the trust then lift from the property and shift to the proceeds of sale (ie the purchase money).

Once overreaching has taken place, any beneficiary under a trust no longer has an interest in the property. Their interest is in the proceeds of sale. The buyer, therefore, takes the property free of the trust interest.

Overreaching is only effective for beneficial interests under a trust. It *cannot* be used in respect of any other third party interest.

Overreaching applies to both unregistered and registered land. When considering a set of facts, consider:

(i) What stage has the transaction reached? If completion has not yet occurred, the buyer can ask the seller to appoint a second trustee in order to overreach.

(ii) If completion has taken place, who did the buyer pay the capital money to? Was it one or two (or more) trustees?

9.2.2 Unregistered land

Where the property has been conveyed to more than one legal owner, the conveyance may contain an express declaration of trust. In the absence of an express declaration, follow the approach set out in **2.2.3** to calculate how the property is held.

In relation to the beneficial owners, (if overreaching has not taken place) the doctrine of notice applies (s 199 LPA 1925). The buyer will be bound unless they are a bona fide purchaser of the legal estate for value without notice (Equity's Darling) (see **Chapter 7** at **7.3.4**).

Example 9.1

In 1989, Russell and Amanda purchased an unregistered parcel of land at 42 Stratford Way ('the Property'). The Property was conveyed to them as express joint tenants in equity. Last year, Amanda mortgaged her interest in the Property to help repay her credit card debts. Her aunt recently died and left her a sizeable gift which allowed Amanda to repay the mortgage. Last month, Russell died. In his will he left his entire estate to his sister, Joan.

Amanda wishes to sell the Property. Would a buyer be bound by any trust interests which may subsist in the Property?

Comment

Initially, the legal estate was held by Russell and Amanda as joint tenants. Upon his death, the right of survivorship applies, therefore, Amanda survives Russell and becomes the sole trustee.

Initially, the equitable interest was held as a joint tenancy due to the express declaration. This was severed when Amanda mortgaged her interest - the act of one party operating on their share. Therefore, Amanda and Russell held the equity as tenants in common in equal shares.

When Russell died, he was a tenant in common. His share in the Property, therefore, passes to his sister, Joan, via his will; meaning Amanda and Joan hold as tenants in common in equal shares.

A buyer would take free of the beneficial interests under the trust if they pay the capital monies to a minimum of two trustees. In order to achieve this, Amanda would need to appoint a second trustee.

If the beneficial interest under the trust is not overreached, the buyer would be bound by the interest unless they were Equity's Darling - a bona fide purchase of the legal estate for value without notice.

9.2.3 Registered land

The beneficiary under a trust should protect their interest by placing a restriction in the proprietorship register (s 40 LRA 2002). Entry of a restriction will prevent the registration of a later registrable disposition for value which is not in accordance with the terms of the restriction.

Where the property is held as beneficial joint tenants, there will be no restriction in the proprietorship register. This is because, if a co-owner dies, the right of survivorship means that their interest in the property automatically passes to the surviving co-owner(s), whether or not they have a will.

Conversely, where the property is held as tenants in common in equity, a restriction should appear in the proprietorship register warning a buyer of the need to pay their purchase money to a minimum of two trustees. On the death of one tenant in common in equity, their interest passes to their estate (to be dealt with by their will or the rules of intestacy). So, if there were originally two tenants in common, the seller will need to appoint a second trustee. However, if there are at least two surviving tenants in common, no further action need be taken.

If overreaching has not taken place (and there is no restriction), the beneficiary under a trust may have the protection of an overriding interest under Sch 3, para 2 LRA, provided that at the date of the disposition to the purchaser (widely defined) there is:

- obvious occupation on a reasonably careful inspection of the land; or
- the buyer has actual knowledge of the interest; and
- the beneficiary under the trust has disclosed their interest on enquiry (when reasonably expected to do so).

See **Chapter 8, 8.7** and **8.9**.

Example 9.2

Kim purchased 14 Sidney Mews ('the Property') from the registered freehold proprietor, Ray. Kim moved into the Property yesterday to find that John was refusing to leave. John (Ray's long-term partner) moved into the Property five years ago on the understanding that it would be his and Ray's 'forever home'. John used the sale proceeds from his previous house to extend and renovate the Property.

Will Kim be bound by John's interest (if any) in the Property?

Comment

On the facts, John and Ray are not married or civil partners, and therefore home rights under s 30 FLA 1996 do not apply.

There is evidence of an understanding between Ray and John (the Property would be their forever home). John has acted to his detriment in reliance on that understanding (he sold his previous house and used the proceeds to extend and renovate the Property). John may have a beneficial interest under a constructive trust.

A constructive trust is equitable and there are no formalities for its creation.

John should have registered a restriction in the proprietorship register. This would warn Kim of the need to appoint a second trustee in order to overreach John's interest. Overreaching has not occurred as Kim has paid the purchase money to Ray alone.

John's interest may be overriding under Sch 3, para 2. He holds a proprietary interest (a beneficial interest under a trust) and he is clearly in occupation at the date of the disposition (he is refusing to leave). Kim would be bound by the overriding interest.

Summary – trusts (express or implied)

Unregistered land	**Registered land**
The interest is overreached if the purchase money is paid to a minimum of two trustees.	The interest is overreached if the purchase money is paid to a minimum of two trustees.
If not overreached, the doctrine of notice applies.	If not overreached, a restriction will prevent the purchaser from being registered.
	The interest may be overriding under Sch 3, para 2 LRA 2002.

9.2.4 Home rights

Section 30 of the FLA 1996 created 'home rights'. This is a statutory right of occupation of the matrimonial home for a non-owning spouse or civil partner. Non-owning means not holding the legal estate. The right arises provided that:

(a) the parties are legally married or civil partners (and not divorced); and

(b) the home is, has been or is intended to be the matrimonial home.

Home rights do not create an interest in land.

Home rights exist independently of any equitable interest arising under a trust (whether express or implied).

Unregistered land

A home right must be protected by registration of a class F Land Charge (s 2 LCA 1972). If so protected, the Land Charge is deemed to be actual notice and, therefore, binding on the buyer (s 198 LPA 1925). If not so protected, a Land Charge is void against a buyer for money or money's worth of any interest unless the Land Charge is registered before completion of the purchase.

Registered land

A home right must be protected by entry of a notice in the charges register (ss 29 and 32 LRA 2002).

An unprotected home right *cannot* take effect as an overriding interest as it has been specifically excluded from the effect of Sch 3, para 2 by s 31(1)(b) FLA 1996.

Summary – home rights

Unregistered land	Registered land
Class F Land Charge.	Notice in the charges register. **Cannot** be an overriding interest – s 31(10)(b) FLA 1996.

9.3 Easements (Chapter 3)

An easement will be binding as between the original owners of the dominant and servient tenements. When the servient tenement is sold, will the buyer be bound by the easement? The answer depends upon how and when the easement was created.

9.3.1 Unregistered land

A legal easement (whether created expressly, by necessity, common intention, the rule in *Wheeldon v Burrows*, s 62 LPA 1925 or by prescription) is binding against the whole world. This means that the buyer will be bound by it.

An equitable easement created post-1926 will only bind the buyer if it has been protected as a D(iii) Land Charge (s 2 LCA 1972). If so protected, the Land Charge is deemed to be actual notice and, therefore, binding on the buyer (s 198 LPA 1925). If not so protected, a Land Charge is void against a buyer for money or money's worth of a legal estate unless the Land Charge is registered before completion of the purchase.

An equitable easement created pre-1926 is protected by the equitable doctrine of notice. The buyer is bound unless they are a bona fide purchaser of the legal estate for value without notice (Equity's Darling).

See **9.3.2(d)** for how equitable easements are created.

Summary – unregistered land

Type of easement	How protected
Legal easement	Binding against the whole world
Equitable easement pre-1926	The doctrine of notice applies
Equitable easement post-1926	Must be protected by registration of a D(iii) Land Charge

9.3.2 Registered land

The treatment of easements in registered land is somewhat complex. How an easement is protected depends upon:

- when it was created; and
- how it was created.

This will be dealt with as follows:

(a) easements and profits existing before 12 October 2003;
(b) express legal easements and profits expressly created after 12 October 2003;
(c) legal easements and profits created by implication or prescription after 12 October 2003; and
(d) equitable easements and profits created after 12 October 2003.

(a) Easements and profits existing before 12 October 2003

All legal easements and profits, equitable profits and equitable easements ('openly exercised and enjoyed') retain their status as overriding interests under s 70(1)(a) LRA 1925 (as interpreted by the Court of Appeal in *Thatcher v Douglas* (1996) 146 NLJ 282 in the case of equitable easements). They continue to be overriding interests under Sch 12 LRA 2002.

(b) Express legal easements and profits expressly created after 12 October 2003

All new expressly created grants or reservations of legal easements and profits are registrable dispositions and have to be completed by registration – s 27(2)(d) LRA 2002. This means any easement or profit created by deed after 12 October 2003.

When the grant or reservation is registered notices are automatically put on the charges register of the burdened land (and entries made in the property register of the benefited land if the benefited land is also registered land).

If the easement or profit is not completed by registration, it will take effect only as an equitable easement.

(c) Legal easements and profits created by implication or prescription after 12 October 2003

Such easements/profits do not require a deed in order to be legal and can be implied by:

- necessity;
- common intention;
- *Wheeldon v Burrows*;
- s 62 LPA 1925.

Or created by prescription.

They will take effect as overriding interests if one of the three conditions is satisfied in Sch 3, para 3 LRA 2002 as at the date of the disposition to the buyer:

(i) the purchaser has actual knowledge of the easement or profit; or

(ii) the existence of the right would have been apparent on a reasonably careful inspection of the land over which the easement or profit is exercisable; *or*

(iii) the easement or profit has been exercised at least once in the year prior to the disposition.

(d) **Equitable easements and profits created after 12 October 2003**

Equitable easements and profits can arise in three ways:

(i) an easement or profit has been expressly and validly created by deed post-2003 but is not completed by registration in accordance with s 27(2)(d) LRA 2002. Therefore, the easement or profit is effectively demoted to an equitable right; or

(ii) there has been an attempt to expressly create a legal easement or profit but not in the form of deed. Therefore, the right would be recognised in equity based on the *Walsh v Lonsdale* principle; or

(iii) an easement or profit has been created for an uncertain duration which does not comply with the criteria set out in s 1(2)(a) LPA 1925 (ie an easement for life). Therefore, the easement or profit is effectively demoted to an equitable right.

Section 27(2)(d) and Sch 3, para 3 LRA 2002 relate to legal easements and profits only, therefore, equitable easements are neither registrable dispositions nor overriding interests.

Equitable easements and profits only bind a buyer if the person with the benefit of the interest (ie the owner of the dominant tenement) has entered a notice on the charges register of the servient/burdened land - ss 29 and 32 LRA 2002. In order to bind a purchaser (widely defined), the notice must be registered prior to the registration of any disposition of a registered estate for valuable consideration (s 29 LRA 2002).

In the absence of a notice, an easement cannot be upgraded to overriding status under Sch 3, para 2 - *Chaudhary v Yavuz* [2011] EWCA Civ 1314. The dominant owner had failed to protect an equitable easement by notice and then argued that such an easement should be protected as a proprietary interest in land with actual occupation as per Sch 3, para 2. The court found that exercise of an easement was a 'mere user' of land and not 'actual occupation'.

Example 9.3

Marcel has recently purchased the freehold registered title to 52 Lark Rise ('the Property') and upon moving in has discovered the following:

(a) Agnes, who lives at 54 Lark Rise, has been using a shortcut every Tuesday across the Property to reach the village hall for her Women's Institute meeting since 1985; and

(b) Gavin, who owns 50 Lark Rise, produces a deed dated 2004 stating that he may connect into and use the drains beneath the Property.

Is Marcel bound by either of these easements?

Comment

(a) **Agnes' shortcut**

The facts state Agnes lives at 54 Lark Rise but not whether she is the freehold owner. If she is a tenant, then she cannot acquire prescriptive rights.

Assuming that Agnes is the freehold owner, she has exercised the right continuously (once a week) and as of right (nothing in the facts to suggest otherwise) for over 20 years creating an easement by prescription.

As such, the easement is protected as an overriding interest under Sch 3, para 3 LRA 2002 provided one of the criteria are met (see **9.3.2(c)(i)–(iii)**). Here, the right has been used at least once in the year preceding the disposition to Marcel. This means that Marcel is bound by the easement.

(b) **Gavin's drains**

The easement of drainage was expressly granted by deed; therefore, creating a legal easement. It was created after the implementation of the LRA 2002 and is, therefore, a registrable disposition under s 27(2)(d) LRA 2002. If the easement is not completed by registration, it will exist in equity only. An equitable easement cannot be upgraded to an overriding interest under Sch 3, para 2.

Therefore, the easement of drainage will only bind Marcel if it is protected by registration.

Summary – easements and profits in registered land

Date created	**Method of creation**	**Method of protection**
Pre-2003	Legal easements and profits, equitable profits and equitable easements (which are openly exercised and enjoyed).	Retain overriding status under Sch 12 LRA 2002
Post-2003	Easements and profits, expressly created by deed.	Registrable dispositions which must be completed by registration in order to be legal – s 27(2)(d) LRA 2002
Post-2003	Legal easements (and profits to the extent that they can be so created) created by necessity, common intention, *Wheeldon v Burrows*, s 62 LPA 1925 and prescription. **NB** does not include express legal easements.	As an overriding interest in Sch 3, para 3, provided one of the criteria is met.
Post-2003	An equitable easement.	Entry of a notice in the charges register. The right cannot be upgraded to overriding status under Sch 3, para 2 LRA 2002.

9.4 Freehold covenants (Chapter 4)

The burden of a freehold covenant only runs in equity if the requirements in *Tulk v Moxhay* are satisfied:

(a) the covenant must be negative in substance;

(b) the covenant must, at the time of the creation of the covenant, have been made to benefit dominant land retained by the covenantee;

(c) the covenant must touch and concern the dominant land;

(d) the covenant must be made with the intent to burden the servient land; and

(e) the owner of the servient land must have notice of the covenant for it to bind them.

A purchaser (widely defined) of the servient land (the land bound by the covenant) will only be bound by the covenant if they have notice of it.

The rules on notice differ between unregistered and registered land.

9.4.1 Unregistered land

Restrictive covenants created before 1926 remain subject to the doctrine of notice. Such covenants bind all, save the bona fide purchaser for value of the legal estate for value without notice ('Equity's Darling').

Post-1926 a restrictive covenant must be protected by registration of a D(ii) Land Charge. The Land Charge must be registered against the name of the estate owner as it appears in the deeds.

Registration of a D(ii) Land Charge is deemed to constitute actual notice of the interest as from the date of registration. If not so protected, a Land Charge is void against a buyer for money or money's worth of a legal estate unless the Land Charge is registered before completion of the purchase.

Example 9.4

In 1985, Hening, the freehold owner of 2 and 4 Coventry Street, sells number 4 ('the Property') to Sally (by deed) subject to a covenant by Sally to only use the Property as a private dwelling house. In 1988, Sally sold the Property to Giles. Giles now wishes to use the Property as a children's nursery.

Is Giles bound by the covenant?

Comment

Sally appears to have entered into a restrictive covenant to only use the property as a private dwelling house.

A restrictive covenant is equitable by nature. Restrictive covenants must be created by writing and signed. A deed would more than meet this requirement.

The burden of a restrictive covenant cannot run at common law and will only run in equity if the conditions in *Tulk v Moxhay* are met:

(a) the covenant must be negative in substance (it is as it requires no effort or expenditure for its performance);

(b) the covenant must, at the time of the creation of the covenant, have been made to benefit dominant land retained by the covenantee (Hening retained number 2);

(c) the covenant must touch and concern the dominant land (it does as any dominant owner would find it a benefit);

(d) the covenant must be made with the intent to burden the servient land (this is not expressed in the facts, but can be implied by s 79 LPA 1925); and

(e) the owner of the servient land must have notice of the covenant for it to bind them.

If Hening registered a D(ii) Land Charge against Sally's name as it appears in the title deeds, this will constitute actual notice and bind Giles. If the Land Charge has not been registered, then Giles will not be bound by the restrictive covenant as he is a purchaser for money or money's worth of the legal estate.

9.4.2 Registered land

A restrictive covenant is an IARE. By s 29(1) LRA 2002 a purchaser of a registered title for valuable consideration takes free of an unprotected IARE.

A restrictive covenant is protected by registration of a notice in the charges register (s 32 LRA 2002). This can be done without the consent of the registered proprietor. In order to bind a purchaser, it must be entered before the registration of the disposition to the buyer.

A restrictive covenant not protected as a notice is not capable of being an overriding interest under Sch 3, para 2.

Example 9.5

In 2010, Harvey, the freehold registered owner of 2 and 4 Totnes Street, sells number 4 ('the Property') to Marsha (by deed) subject to a covenant by Marsha to only use the Property as a private dwelling house. In 2024, Marsha sold the Property to Ian. Ian wishes to use the Property for his physiotherapy business.

Is Ian bound by the covenant?

Comment

Marsha appears to have entered into a restrictive covenant to only use the property as a private dwelling house.

A restrictive covenant is equitable by nature. Restrictive covenants must be created by writing and signed. A deed would more than meet this requirement.

The burden of a restrictive covenant cannot run at common law and will only run in equity if the conditions in *Tulk v Moxhay* are met:

(a) the covenant must be negative (restrictive) in substance (it is as it requires no effort or expenditure for its performance and restricts the way the land can be used);

(b) the covenant must, at the time of the creation of the covenant, have been made to benefit dominant land retained by the covenantee (Harvey retained number 2);

(c) the covenant must touch and concern the dominant land (it does as any dominant owner would find it a benefit);

(d) the covenant must be made with the intent to burden the servient land (this is not expressed in the facts, but can be implied by s 79 LPA 1925); and

(e) the owner of the servient land must have notice of the covenant for it to bind them.

The restrictive covenant will only bind Ian if it was entered as a notice in the charges register of the title to the Property prior to the date of the disposition to Ian. If it was not so registered, Ian will not be bound by the restrictive covenant.

Summary – restrictive covenants

Unregistered land	Registered land
Class D(ii) Land Charge.	Notice under s 32 appearing in the charges register.

9.5 Mortgages (Chapter 5)

Mortgages are capable of being legal interests in land. A deed is required to create a legal mortgage in relation to a legal estate.

Where the document lacks the requirements of a deed, equity may intervene and recognise an equitable mortgage under the principle in *Walsh v Lonsdale*.

A mortgage can be created over an equitable interest provided it complies with s 53(1) LPA 1925. For example, when a co-owner of land creates a mortgage in relation to their equitable interest under a trust.

The rules for protection of mortgages differ in registered and unregistered land.

9.5.1 Unregistered land

Where a first legal mortgage is created over an unregistered title, s 85(1) LPA 1925 gives lenders the right to take custody of the title deeds. Most lenders will, therefore, take deposit of the title deeds as part of their security. The inability for the borrower to produce their title deeds warns a buyer that there is a mortgage over the property.

A legal mortgage protected by the deposit of deeds is binding against the whole world. Creation of a first mortgage over unregistered land will also trigger compulsory first registration of the title to the land (see s 4 LRA 2002).

A legal mortgage not protected by the deposit of deeds (a puisne mortgage) must be protected by registration of a Class C(i) Land Charge. A puisne mortgage is usually a second or subsequent mortgage.

Registration of a C(i) Land Charge is deemed to constitute actual notice of the interest as from the date of registration. If not so protected, a Land Charge is void against a buyer for valuable consideration of any interest unless the Land Charge is registered before completion of the purchase.

9.5.2 Registered land

A mortgage over a registered title is a registrable disposition under s 27(2)(f) LRA 2002. It will become a legal mortgage only when it is entered in the charges register of the title affected.

Where there is more than one charge registered against the title, the order for priority depends on the order in which they are entered on the register (s 48 LRA 2002) and not the date of creation of the charges. This means that the mortgage that appears first on the title register will rank first (ie be paid first from the proceeds of sale).

A lender will also need to consider whether third party interests are binding on them, for example, when exercising the power of sale:

(i) if the interest was created before the date of registration of the mortgage, then the lender needs to check whether they are bound by the interest; and

(ii) if the interest was created after the date of registration of the mortgage, then the lender is not bound, unless it gave its consent to the creation of the interest (for example the grant of a lease by the borrower).

An interest created prior to the registration of the mortgage will only bind the lender if, in accordance with s 29 LRA 2002, it is:

- a registered charge;
- the subject of a notice in the register; or
- an overriding interest in Sch 3 (note that such interests have to be created prior to the date of completion of the mortgage, not the date of registration).

In relation to any beneficial interest under a trust arising via a contribution to the purchase price, such an interest would only be protected by actual occupation under Sch 3, para 2. Such occupation would need to pre-date the creation (ie completion) of the mortgage in order to bind the lender. This will not usually be the case where the mortgage money is used to acquire the property. The person with the beneficial interest under a trust will only take up occupation after the creation of the mortgage. Their interest will, therefore, not be binding on the lender.

Where the legal owner mortgages the property post-acquisition (or re-mortgages it), then the lender may be bound by any trust interest that already exists (unless the lender has overreached).

Example 9.6

Stephen, the freehold registered owner of Poppy Farm ('the Property') created the following interests:

(i) Five years ago, a first mortgage by deed over the Property in favour of Harry. Harry only registered the charge at Land Registry last month.

(ii) Two years ago, Stephen allowed Rahul to move into the farm house forming part of the Property. Rahul has paid Stephen a rent of £600 per month and continues to live in the farm house.

(iii) Last year, a second mortgage by deed over the Property in favour of Margaret. The charge was duly registered at Land Registry.

Stephen has been struggling financially and has three months of arrears in relation to the mortgage in favour of Margaret.

Margaret would like to exercise the power of sale but would like to know:

- which lender has priority; and
- would the sale be subject to Rahul's occupation of the farm house?

Comment

Although Harry's charge was created first, it will rank second in priority as Margaret's charge was registered first. This means that Margaret would be paid first from the proceeds of sale.

Rahul's potential interest was created before Margaret's charge so Margaret will need to check whether it binds her.

Rahul's interest has the characteristics of a lease:

- permitted duration (monthly tenancy);
- exclusive possession (Rahul lives in the farm house and nothing in the facts to suggest exclusive possession does not exist);
- correct formalities.

The lease is for less than three years, takes effect in possession and there is no fine or premium payable. Provided the rent is the best rent reasonably obtainable, this will be a parol lease (ie a legal lease).

A legal lease for seven years or less is automatically protected as an overriding interest (Sch 3, para 1). Rahul's lease will be binding and any sale by Margaret will be subject to it.

9.6 Leases (Chapter 6)

When there is a disposition of the reversion, will the purchaser be bound? Remember that purchaser is widely defined to include a tenant and a mortgagee.

A lease is capable of being a legal estate. In order to be legal a lease must be created by deed. However, certain legal leases may be created informally if they meet the requirements of s 54(2) LPA 1925 (parol leases). See **6.3.2**.

Equity may intervene and recognise an equitable lease where there has been an attempt to expressly create a lease, but not in the form of a deed following the *Walsh v Lonsdale* principle. See **1.10.3** and **6.3.3**.

A licence does not create a proprietary interest in land and will not bind a purchaser of either unregistered or registered land.

9.6.1 Unregistered land

A legal lease (whether created by deed or by parol) is binding against the whole world. This means that the buyer is bound by it.

An equitable lease created post-1926 will only bind the buyer if it has been protected as an estate contract C(iv) Land Charge (s 2 LCA 1972). If so protected, the Land Charge is deemed to be actual notice and, therefore, binding on the buyer (s 198 LPA 1925). If not so protected, a Land Charge is void against a buyer for money or money's worth of a legal estate unless the Land Charge is registered before completion of the purchase.

An equitable lease created pre-1926 is protected by the equitable doctrine of notice. The buyer is bound unless they are a bona fide purchaser of the legal estate for value without notice ('Equity's Darling').

Example 9.7

Matilda is the freehold owner of a three storey office building ('the Property'). She creates the following:

(i) three years ago, a lease (by deed) for a term of five years over the first storey of the Property in favour of Oliver; and

(ii) two years ago, a lease (not in the form of a deed) for a term of 10 years over the second storey of the Property in favour of Alice.

Matilda wishes to assign the freehold reversion to Peter.

Will Peter be bound by Oliver or Alice's interests?

Comment

Taking each interest in turn:

Oliver

The lease was created by deed and is, therefore, a legal lease. This is binding against the whole world and will bind Peter.

Alice

The lease lacks the formality of a deed. Equity may intervene to recognise this as an equitable lease if there is:

- a contract;
- complying with s 2 LPMPA 1989; and
- Alice seeks equity with clean hands.

A post-1926 equitable lease must be protected as a Class C(iv) Land Charge prior to the disposition to Peter in order to be binding. If not so protected, Peter will take free of the interest.

If the lease does not comply with the terms of an equitable lease, it may be a legal monthly periodic tenancy on the basis of Alice's exclusive possession and payment of the rent. This would be a legal parol lease binding on Peter as it is good against the whole world.

Summary – unregistered land

Type of lease	Method of protection
Legal lease	Binding against the whole world
Pre-1926 Equitable lease	The doctrine of notice
Post-1926 Equitable lease	Must be protected by registration of a C(iv) Land Charge

9.6.2 Registered land

The protection for legal leases depends on the duration of the lease.

(a) **Legal leases for more than seven years**

A legal lease granted for more than seven years is a registrable disposition and has to be completed by registration – s 27(2)(b)(i) LRA 2002.

The lease will have its own title number and register. It will also appear in the charges register of the landlord's title within the schedule of leases as it burdens the landlord's title.

If the lease is not completed by registration, it will it take effect only as an equitable lease.

(b) **Legal leases for seven years or less**

Legal leases for seven years or less are automatically protected as overriding interests by Sch 3, para 1. This applies to fixed-term leases and periodic tenancies (provided the period is not more than seven years). See **8.8.1**.

(c) **Equitable leases**

An equitable lease can be created in one of two ways:

(i) A legal lease for more than seven years has not been registered in accordance with s 27(2)(b)(i) LRA 2002; or

(ii) There has been an attempt to expressly create a legal lease but not in the form of deed, therefore, the right would be recognised in equity based on the *Walsh v Lonsdale* principle. See **1.10.3**.

Equitable leases are protected by entry of a notice in the charges register (ss 29 and 32 LRA 2002). In order to bind a purchaser (widely defined), the notice must be registered prior to the registration of the disposition to the buyer.

If the equitable lease is not protected by entry of a notice, the interest may take effect as an overriding interest under Sch 3, para 2 provided at the date of the disposition to the buyer (widely defined) there is:

- obvious actual occupation; or
- the buyer has actual knowledge of the interest; or
- the tenant failed to disclose their interest on enquiry (when reasonably expected to do so).

See **8.9.**

Example 9.8

Harriet is the freehold registered proprietor of 36 Harbour Lane ('the Property'). Last year, Harriet granted a 10-year lease (by deed) to Monica. Monica immediately moved into the Property and has paid the monthly rent of £700 ever since.

Harriet has now sold the Property to Tom, who is shocked to discover that Monica is still living in the Property as there was nothing in the registered title to suggest a lease existed. Tom recalls seeing Monica when he inspected the Property prior to completion. Tom assumed that Monica was a friend of Harriet's and would leave on the completion of the sale.

Is Tom bound by Monica's lease?

Comment

The lease has all the essential characteristics of a lease with a permitted duration (10 years), exclusive possession (nothing in the facts to suggest otherwise) and was created by deed.

A legal lease for 10 years is a registrable disposition and, therefore, must be completed by registration in order to be legal (s 27 LRA 2002). This has not happened as there is nothing in the registered freehold title.

If not so registered, the lease can only take effect in equity. An equitable lease must be protected by entry of a notice in the charges register (ss 29 and 32 LRA 2002). Again, this has not happened as there was no mention of the lease in the title to the Property.

The equitable lease may be protected by Monica's occupation as an overriding interest under Sch 3, para 2. The facts state that Monica remains in occupation and her occupation was obvious to Tom when he inspected the Property prior to the disposition to him. The overriding interest will not appear in the register but, nonetheless, is binding on Tom.

Summary registered land

Type of lease	How protected
Legal lease for more than seven years	Registrable disposition under s 27(2)(b)(i) LRA 2002
Legal lease for seven years or less	Automatically protected as an overriding interest under Sch 3, para 1
Equitable lease	Protected by entry of a notice in the charges register. If not so protected, the interest may be overriding under Sch 3, para 2 LRA 2002.

Summary

In order to analyse whether or not an interest is binding on a third party buyer follow these steps:

- Identify the interest.
- Is the interest capable of being legal, or is it equitable by nature?
- Have the correct formalities been used?
- If the interest is capable of being legal, but there is no deed, will equity intervene?
- Identify whether the interest is legal, equitable or statutory (ie home rights).

- How should the right be protected in unregistered or registered land?
- Has the interest been protected? If a beneficial interest under a trust has overreaching happened?
- If registered land, could an unprotected equitable interest be upgraded to overriding status under Sch 3, para 2?

Sample questions

Question 1

A solicitor is acting for a purchaser of a registered freehold property. The seller tells the buyer that the property is burdened by an easement granted by deed in 2006. What will the buyer's solicitor look for when examining the official copy of the title to the property to confirm that the easement is properly registered?

A An entry referring to an easement in the charges register.

B A restriction on dealing in the proprietorship register.

C An entry referring to an easement in the property register.

D An entry referring to a restrictive covenant in the charges register.

E An entry referring to an easement in the proprietorship register.

Answer

The correct option is A.

The easement was expressly created by deed after October 2003 and is, therefore, a registrable disposition. As the easement burdens the property, it would appear in the charges register. Options B, D and E are, therefore, wrong.

An easement would appear in the property register only if it benefited the property. This is not the case on the facts. Option C is, therefore, wrong.

Question 2

A solicitor acts for the buyer of an unregistered property. Last year, the seller granted the adjoining owner the right (by deed) to use their property as a shortcut to reach the nearby village for a period of 10 years.

Which of the following best describes the buyer's position in relation to this interest?

A The buyer will not be bound by the interest as it is for a fixed duration and, therefore, not a legal easement.

B The buyer will not be bound by the interest unless it has been registered as a D(iii) Land Charge.

C The buyer will be bound by the legal interest as it is binding against the whole world.

D The buyer will not be bound unless the easement has been registered on the seller's title.

E The buyer will be bound as they have notice of the easement under the doctrine of notice.

Answer

The correct option is C.

The interest is an easement. An easement must be equivalent to a freehold (forever) or a term of years absolute (a fixed ascertainable duration). The period of 10 years complies with this. Therefore, option A is wrong.

An easement is capable of being legal but, in order to be legal, must (unless created by implication or prescription) be created by deed. The facts state that this is the case. In unregistered land a legal easement is binding against the whole world.

A D(iii) Land Charge protects an equitable easement. The easement is legal. Therefore, option B is wrong.

The doctrine of notice applies only to equitable easements. Option E is, therefore, wrong.

Option D is wrong as it relates to registered land and the question relates to unregistered land.

Question 3

A married couple purchase a registered freehold property with the help of the wife's parents. The parents contributed half the purchase price and occupy the property. One year after their purchase, the married couple obtain a loan in return for the grant of a mortgage in favour of a lender. The married couple default on the loan and the lender seeks to exercise its power of sale.

Is the lender bound by the interests of the wife's parents?

A Yes, the wife's parents have an overriding interest which is binding on the lender.

B Yes, the wife's parents have actual occupation which is binding on the lender.

C Yes, because the lender has failed to overreach the wife's parents' interest.

D No, because the occupation by the parents occurred after the mortgage was created.

E No, because the lender has overreached the parents' beneficial interest under a trust.

Answer

The correct option is E.

The lender paid capital money to two trustees (the married couple). This had the effect of lifting the beneficial interests of the parents (as a consequence of their contribution to the purchase price) from the property and to the proceeds of sale (ie the loan advance from the lender). Option C is, therefore, wrong.

Option A is wrong because although the parents may have a beneficial interest under a trust protected as an overriding interest, such an interest has been overreached by the lender.

Option B is wrong as occupation alone does not create an overriding interest. This must be coupled with a proprietary interest in land.

Option D is wrong because the facts clearly indicate that the parents were in occupation prior to the advance by the lender.

Index